A COMMON
HUMAN
GROUND

A COMMON HUMAN GROUND

Universality and Particularity in a Multicultural World

Claes G. Ryn

University of Missouri Press
Columbia

Copyright © 2003 by
The Curators of the University of Missouri
University of Missouri Press, Columbia, Missouri 65211
Printed and bound in the United States of America
All rights reserved
First paperback printing, 2019

Library of Congress Cataloging-in-Publication Data

Ryn, Claes G., 1943-
A common human ground : universality and
particularity in a multicultural world / Claes G. Ryn.
p.   cm.
Includes bibliographical references and index.
ISBN 978-0-8262-1494-2 (paperback : alk. paper)
ISBN 978-0-8262-2203-9 (hardcover : alk. paper)
1. Philosophical anthropology.   2. Universals
(Philosophy)   3. Ethnic relations.   I. Title.
BD450 .R96 2003
303.48'2—dc22   2003012644

⊗™   This paper meets the requirements of the
American National Standard for Permanence of Paper
for Printed Library Materials, Z39.48, 1984.

Designer: Stephanie Foley
Typeface: Bembo

Contents

Preface to the Paperback Edition

At the beginning of the twenty-first century large and seemingly irreconcilable social and political trends in the West and elsewhere seemed to signal an era of progressive fragmentation, tension, and conflict. No deeply grounded harmonizing influences were discernible that might supply cultural and other cohesion comparable to that provided by the once vigorous classical and Christian traditions in Western civilization and by corresponding traditions in other parts of the world. The centralizing, homogenizing forces of globalization were generating little more than a superficial technological and economic commonality, as in the so-called European Community. At the same time, chiefly in the Western world, the doctrine of "multiculturalism" encouraged a push for diversity and facilitated a proliferation of often conflicting group interests. These developments added to the disrupting effects of a cultural radicalism that challenged old beliefs and practices as authoritarian and oppressive of women and minorities. In societies already exhibiting deep religious, moral, intellectual, political, and economic fissures, globalization generated protests and efforts to reassert older national and regional identities.

It was in 2000 that the lectures on which *A Common Human Ground* is based were given at Beijing University. Since then the signs of division have kept multiplying. In the West, large-scale migration from culturally alien parts of the world has added to social fragmentation and undermined cultural cohesion. Deeds of terror and spreading violence have eroded an older sense of stability and security. The multiculturalist assumption that diversity is a value in itself and poses no significant threat to social order rings more and more hollow. It is sharply contradicted by growing claims, some no less extreme than radical multiculturalism, that order requires cultural unity. Eruptions of "nationalism" are due not only to centralizing and globalizing forces having eroded national sovereignty, but to attacks on cherished historically evolved beliefs and practices. The vote in Great Britain to leave the European Union was but one prominent example of resistance to distant and central authority perceived as insensitive or hostile to valued national and regional identities.

All over the Western world deepening dissatisfaction with overall trends has generated popular protest movements that sharply challenge entrenched political, journalistic, intellectual, and cultural elites. These elites have used the term "populism" to describe opposition to their leadership. They have portrayed "populists" as irresponsible, opportunistic, and demagogic, which implies that those making the charges have none of the mentioned weaknesses. But the "populists" have been reacting to what *they* see as irresponsible, opportunistic, and demagogic rule. Leaving aside who might have the better argument, what the so-called populists have in common is that they are perceived by the established elites as more than marginally challenging their authority and as attracting widespread popular support. The attempts by established elites to disparage oppositional groups have failed to conceal that the authority of the elites is crumbling. All over the Western world millions upon millions of people are fundamentally questioning the direction of their societies, while those accustomed to ruling are responding with condescension and intense efforts to hold on to power.

In the United States the election of Donald Trump to the presidency revealed the depth and strength of popular dissatisfaction with the established order, but the reigning elites simply refused to accept this brash interloper, who bluntly threatened their right to dominate. His election triggered a protracted constitutional crisis. Getting rid of Trump became for large segments of America's leadership class an obsession. The United States Constitution, long the pride of Americans, was barely holding.

One of President Trump's violations of America's post–World War II consensus was to question the assumption, viewed as almost self-evident in the foreign policy establishment, that the United States must preside over and guarantee world order. During his election campaign Trump signaled a policy of "America first" and a desire to move away from interventionism and nation-building, which aroused great hostility in the foreign policy establishment. The fact that President Trump then surrounded himself with hawkish foreign policy advisers long committed to the very posture he had criticized raised questions about the depth and consistency of his beliefs, and contributed to a general feeling of confusion and disarray.

One has to ask whether, in the long run, the kind of dissonance and fragmentation prevalent all over the Western world is compatible with social and political cohesion. The tension among key actors and centers of opinion and the incidence of open hostilities and violence are ominous. There seems to be in Western society at the same time no emerging deeper consensus, no obvious new sources for allaying division that can replace old ones.

The slogan of the French Revolution of 1789, "freedom, equality, and brotherhood," might be used as a convenient summary of what were to be sources of unity in the Western world after the detested old traditions had been uprooted. Today that slogan has a distinctly ironical, even satirical ring. Freedom in the sense of liberation from ancient beliefs and institutions produced certain fairly stable liberal institutions and practices, but only when it incorporated major elements of the old order. In the hands of the most radical and committed advocates of liberation, "freedom" produced totalitarian regimes that enslaved and killed millions.

The ideal of equality, though embraced by progressives everywhere, proved elusive except as modified by old traditions. As for its most radical iterations, they were easily overpowered by other human motives, which produced sharp economic divisions and other polarization. No societies were ever more dedicated to the ideal of equality than the Soviet Union and Communist China, but in practice they became highly stratified, rigidly structured caste societies. So-called capitalist societies never aspired to equality except in the most limited sense, but generated such huge disparities in wealth and influence as to breed widespread resentment and other social division.

The brotherhood of man continues to color the rhetoric of progressive reformers, but has come up against a very different historical reality. You might have thought that in the twentieth century the brotherhood of man with its dreamy sentimentalism would finally have been abandoned as an unattainable goal, a grand illusion. That century was full of talk of brotherhood and other ideals, but some of those who were most staunchly devoted to those ideals were also among the most ruthless murderers that humanity has seen—Stalin and Mao most prominent among them. The supposedly idealistic and enlightened twentieth century saw more mass killing and inhumanity than any other in history.

The faith in democracy that has usually been closely connected to dreams of freedom, equality, and brotherhood remains a staple of Western rhetoric, but democracy, supposedly a vehicle for the will of the people and a source of social unity and the common good, has proved strongly susceptible to egregious partisanship and demagoguery. Rule by the People has also, in practice, provided cover for elites to manipulate opinion.

Freedom, equality, and brotherhood, purportedly sources of modern order and unity, thus seem today to be little more than decorative symbols. In fact, they draw attention to the sharp contrast between stated goals and historical reality. All too plainly, the old classical and Christian traditions that for long periods gave some coherence and purpose to Western society have reached an advanced state of disrepair. A striking illustration is the condition of the Roman Catholic Church. Long regarded as a source of stability, unity, and order, this institution has been rocked to the core by revelations of egregious crime, debauchery, callousness, and hypocrisy within the clergy. That the clerical hierarchy of one of the most traditional branches of Christianity should have suffered a precipitous loss of moral-spiritual authority and face a virtual rebellion from the laity suggests profound moral-spiritual problems. The depth and scope of this corruption, extending in varying forms to other branches of Christianity, indicates that the religious traditions of Western civilization are floundering.

Societies outside of the Western world have their own sometimes serious problems of order, but, by virtue of the West's long-standing military, political, and economic dominance combined with several centuries of colonialism, these societies, too, have to contend with repercussions of these Western developments. All of this division and attendant insecurity and uncertainty presents societies with great domestic difficulties. Yet, given their potential for inflicting large-scale human suffering, the implications for international relations within and among the old civilizations is an even more important subject.

Threats to order and peace there will always be. That is human life. But stress and dissension of the scope and depth here discussed give urgency to the need for mitigating tensions and holding societies together. Dangerous as the current unsettled and unsettling state of affairs is, it offers an opportunity to question conventional formulas for peace and order. The time is ripe, even overripe, for reexamining common assumptions regarding their sources.

To deal adequately with the problem of order and disorder, unity and diversity, is ultimately to deal with the large ancient philosophical problem of universality and particularity. The polarity in question has many facets, and the meanings of the terms vary according to context and from thinker to thinker. As employed in traditional discourse, the distinction is usually roughly the same as that between transcendence and immanence. Universality and transcendence refer to a more than subjective force for good that opposes the disruptive infinite diversity of individual phenomena. Plato thought of this polarity as the One and the Many. He associated the former with order and meaning, the latter with disorder and meaninglessness. For good to be realized, a transcendent standard had to be respected and diversity reduced to a minimum. This book advances a very different understanding of the two.

To ask how persons, peoples, and civilizations might achieve peaceful and even respectful relations is in the end to ask about the meaning of universality and particularity, which is the same as asking how they are related. The thesis of this book is that universality and particularity can coexist—and more than coexist. Indeed, diversity *of a certain kind* can be shown to *serve* unity and order, be indistinguishable from universality. That is to say that the argument presented here concerning relations among human beings and concerning the problem of order significantly revises common notions of universality and particularity. Particularity is here not understood as necessarily inimical to or different from a higher good. Destructive and vile as particularity can be, it is, in a special sense, also indispensable to universality, in fact, potentially an expression of it. Universality and particularity can come together in synthesis, and, in a sense, become one and the same. The argument advanced in these pages will therefore strike many readers, at least initially, as self-contradictory or at best paradoxical. The reason for that reaction is that an ancient principle of merely abstract logic—the principle of so-called noncontradiction—has been permitted to overrule the actual human experience of universality and particularity. The thesis of this book includes a fundamental change in how the two terms are understood.

A Common Human Ground is about the problem of unity and diversity in all human interaction, but its thesis is developed with special reference to international relations. It formulates the philosophical basis for a new way of thinking about that subject. In so doing it questions common assumptions. It examines dimensions of international relations that are usually ignored by mainstream scholars. The book concentrates on the philosophical crux of the proposed thesis, leaving it to experts in national security, diplomacy, trade, and other fields to explore the implications for those subjects.

The issue of unity and diversity could not bear more directly on problems of politics and statesmanship. Dealing with diversity is an integral and inescapable part of what statesmen must routinely do. They must act in diverse and changeable circumstances and take many competing interests into account, both in political practice and when thinking strategically. Statesmanship of the highest order sometimes requires great creativity and surprising action, an ability, for example, to forge unexpected coalitions or agreements. But for negotiations, cooperation, and generally peaceful relations to be possible, some balance between universality and particularity has to be already present or within reach.

According to the British statesman and thinker Edmund Burke (1729–1797), order requires that a check on will and appetite be placed somewhere. Irresponsibility and ruthlessness must be contained. The less self-restraint that human beings are able to impose on themselves, within, the more restraint and order have to be imposed from without. Do, then, the current circumstances of growing dissension and fragmentation have to be managed by means of overwhelming external force?

In the Western world many believe that the United States must exercise uncontested global leadership. These commentators believe that, to ensure the kind of world order that they favor, America must counteract any challenge to its military and political supremacy. This approach to international order makes many others profoundly and justifiably uncomfortable. It reveals not only an inordinate desire for power but a utopian imagination and great conceit. Yet the problem of order has to be addressed in an international as well as a domestic context.

What about domestic threats to order? Must authoritarian rule ensure stability there as well? If that prospect is unappealing, how to forestall it? What could alleviate the need for external regimentation? Are there adequate nonauthoritarian, "inner" sources of order? The lectures on which this book is based were written because it seemed that scholars addressing the problem of order and peace, including experts in international relations, were not adequately defining the problem. They were virtually ignoring issues that may be central to averting disorder and conflict.

In the field of international relations liberal internationalists and humanitarians have proposed softer, less aggressive versions of American hegemony, but their notions of order certainly are not free of the conceited belief—so marked in the more hawkish globalist interventionists—that the world can and should be reconstructed according to their own notions of what is desirable. The softer, more "idealistic" globalists look to putatively enlightened rationality or sentimental brotherhood of man as sources of peace, but these globalists are, when resisted, not disinclined to use military might to implement their plans for the world. A common brand of such "idealism" is so-called democratic peace theory, the notion that democracies by their very nature are peaceful and conducive to international peace. Proponents of this theory, too, are impatient with opposition and prepared to overcome it through military action if necessary. In theory, the world order that idealistic internationalists favor is one to which they think humanity is naturally predisposed, but, in practice, this proper order becomes something to be imposed on recalcitrant rulers by people who know what is best for mankind.

These and similarly "progressive" and "idealistic" approaches to the problem of order are challenged by so-called realists, who, understandably, think of themselves as more hard-nosed, better equipped to understand the power realities of politics. Realists substitute for what they regard as quasi-utopian wishful thinking and imprudent interventionism a coolheaded, more "clinical" amoralism.

But we are not restricted to a choice between progressive, idealistic expectations and amoral analysis of power relations. What is most commonly called realism in international relations theory is not as realistic as its proponents think. Genuine realism requires a subtle, multifaceted view of what makes human beings tick, for good or ill. It requires an acute awareness of the darker side of human nature but also of the complexity of human motives. Yet mainstream academic theorizing has been prone to simplifying the sources of human action according to some condensed general theory of conduct. A deep prejudice against inquiry into issues of good and evil has steered Western scholars away from what had been the traditional Western view of humanity's moral and cultural predicament. They have largely discarded the ancient belief that human beings are morally cleft between higher and lower potentialities and that self-control, "inner" discipline, is a prerequisite for all but the most superficial and tenuous social order. According to that older Western view, only people of disciplined character can refrain from the egotistical, rash, and ruthless conduct that threatens social cohesion. As Edmund Burke argues, only people who are able to control themselves will reduce the need for authoritarian rule. A central purpose of culture is to assist the moral striving of human beings. Without this striving, not even enlightened egotism will suffice to keep order, leaving that task to brute external force. These are the rudiments of what might be called moral realism.

It is common to view international relations as necessarily involving more conflict than other spheres of human action. So-called realists are prone to the view of Thomas Hobbes that the "war of all against all" characteristic of the state of nature still obtains in the international arena. But, like other mainstream scholars, realists do not attribute this state of affairs, wholly or in part, to some grave moral flaw in human beings that needs to be ameliorated for the sake of peace. They simply regard human beings as by nature self-centered and adopt a semi-mechanistic view of how power can be balanced. Sentimental humanitarians, for their part, lack any deep fears concerning human nature, while rationalists trust in rationality to order the world. Some mainstream scholars hope that well-constructed institutional arrangements will withstand reckless passion. In none of these cases is there a careful weighing of man's moral predicament and of the moral crux of human choice, the struggle between good and evil. According to the supposedly scientific, scholarly mind, moral issues belong to the amorphous sphere of merely subjective speculation.

Mainstream realists may take moral and even religious factors into account, but only to the extent that they are influences relevant to a realist analysis of competing interests and are treated by strictly empirical, sociological methods. In the study of power, no more can or need be said about human motives than that self-interest drives action. Because realists distrust human beings and are even prone to cynicism, they are not as likely as other scholars to engage in wishful thinking, but they fail to recognize the intricacy of human motives and the existence and practical importance of what lies above a simply self-interested pursuit of power. A reductionistic notion of prospective human action makes realist scholars neglect crucial aspects of the problems of order.

A Common Human Ground draws attention to the moral and cultural preconditions for peaceful relations—aspects of the problem of order that mainstream scholars typically ignore, downplay, or finesse. Shunning dreamy idealism, abstract rationalism, and morally neutral realism, the book advances a morally sensitive realism, one that recognizes not only humanity's capacity for enlightened self-interest but a capacity, limited but sometimes crucially important, for transcending pure self-interest. This more fully fledged understanding of man's humanity includes an awareness that chronic human weaknesses are perpetually threatening idealistic dreams, rational designs, clever institutional arrangements, and careful power calculation. For peace and order to achieve any solidity, it is insufficient for these weaknesses to be countered by means of external pressure ranging from law and institutions to military power. Human beings must as far as possible also contain these weaknesses from within, through character, modesty, caution, and circumspection, which presupposes much preparation. Simply put, the ultimate source of either peace or war resides in the heart of human beings. Whatever else a secure peace may require, it presupposes actors whose souls are peaceful. Conversely, the best-laid plans for avoiding war can be nullified in an instant by persons who are belligerent, arrogant, or rash. The moral realism propounded in this book is neither dreamily idealistic, nor rationalistic, nor mechanistic. It is in a way darker and more pessimistic than mainstream academic theories, including realism, but is at the same time more hopeful regarding man's capacity for nobility and regarding its practical efficacy.

The book's overall philosophical thesis applies to all human interaction, ranging from the most intimate and local to that involving governments, but the lectures on which the book is based were written for delivery at Beijing University and put the emphasis on the international dimension of the problem of order. The book advances a philosophy of universality and particularity that is also a philosophy of how persons, peoples, and civilizations might interact peacefully and respectfully. It is an entry in the field of international relations often called grand strategy, but may for that genre, as it currently exists, be a bit of an oddity.

A Common Human Ground provides much of the philosophical rationale for the Center for the Study of Statesmanship (CSS) at the Catholic University of America, which was founded in 2017. The mission of the Center is to explore the ultimate sources of both sound and unsound leadership and to promote wise, farsighted leadership. The Center was started in an attempt to go "upstream" from day-to-day controversies, public policy advocacy, and standard discussion of domestic and international politics in order to examine the often uncritically held views of human nature and the world from which policy preferences stem. By exposing dreamy illusions and other dubious assumptions, the Center seeks to define and foster truly statesmanlike qualities in international and domestic affairs. Statesmanship is leadership out of the ordinary. It is most urgently needed when societies face great challenges. Ordinary leaders may evince opportunism, ignorance, shortsightedness, and recklessness, but statesmen have a capacity in moments of crisis to rise above the passions of the moment, employ a critical historical perspective, see further than others, and pursue not merely partisan advantage but the good of all concerned. The no-more-than-ordinary leader who is in possession of superior power may treat opponents disdainfully and crush them. The statesman, by contrast, knows the deep resentment that such ruthlessness leaves behind and will, whenever possible, seek negotiation and compromise rather than confrontation. All effective leadership requires willpower and shrewdness, but the mark of true statesmanship is that it combines uncompromising realism with respect for a universal human good.

Study of the preconditions of order and peace must recognize the complexities of human life, including the higher potentialities of human existence. It is the entire personality of human beings that predisposes them to either peacefulness or belligerence. One of the purposes of the Center for the Study of Statesmanship, as of this book, is to broaden and deepen the study of human interaction. Specifically, it is essential in exploring the sources of either sound or unsound leadership to understand the great influence of "the culture"—churches, universities, the arts, and entertainment— in setting the direction for society and politics and for individual human beings. Although the mind and especially the *imagination* play decisive roles in shaping the fears and hopes of human beings, and hence their political inclinations, political scientists and other students of human conduct usually make do with incomplete notions of what moves human beings. The Center for the Study of Statesmanship was preceded in the effort to broaden and deepen the understanding of human conduct by the small and independent National Humanities Institute (NHI), founded in 1984. NHI never had the resources to effectively promote its philosophy and intellectual strategy, but it laid much of the intellectual groundwork for the Center for the Study of Statesmanship.

This new edition of *A Common Human Ground* appears at a time when dissonance and division sometimes seem overwhelming. One might well ask how in such circumstances a seemingly delicate moral-cultural commonality that transcends and yet blends with diversity could possibly rein in tension and disorder. It may seem more likely that, increasingly, harsh, authoritarian power will impose its own kind of order both domestically and internationally. But power that is not morally and culturally tamed but descends into confrontation and bullying greatly increases the risk of open conflict. Many hope that enlightened self-interest will protect humanity from calamity, and so it will to some considerable extent. Yet sophisticated self-interest ultimately derives its intuition of what is desirable from a sense, however faint and indirect, of the higher shared humanity that is the subject of this book. Without some awareness of that common human ground, self-interest itself becomes crude, raw, short-sighted, and flimsy—less than enlightened—and easily succumbs to inflamed passion. Unless the moral and cultural preconditions of peace receive urgent and serious attention, humanity may be headed for disasters of unexampled horror.

Preface to the First Edition

This book originated in the "Distinguished Foreign Scholar" lectures that I gave at Beijing University in May of 2000. This lecture series was published in revised and expanded form and in Chinese translation by the same university in 2001 under the title *Unity through Diversity.* The book that is now offered to Western readers has the same structure and general theme, but publication in English has afforded me an opportunity to clarify and extend various points and to add ideas. I have also removed from the text comments and references that were useful to Chinese readers but are dispensable here.

The book's origins will explain its form. To be able to set forth a rather wide-ranging philosophical argument I had to limit the discussion of scholars whose ideas relate in some way to my thesis. Much of the time I restricted myself to comparing my own point of view to general trends of thought with which I agree or disagree. I wanted this English edition to retain the form and flavor of the original lectures and therefore made no major changes in this regard.

Before introducing the subject and argument of the book I should probably try to explain how I came to lecture at Beijing University. It must have been well over a decade ago that I first became aware of interest in my work in China. I received a letter from a scholar at a Chinese university, who asked if I might spare a copy of one of my own books. The letter was written in broken English and on poor-quality stationery. I had no idea of the intellectual seriousness behind the request but fully intended to send the book within a few days. I would have done so, had I not somehow managed to misplace the letter. I simply could not find it. I am all the more angry and embarrassed at my ineptitude because of what I have since learned about interest in my work in China and about the obstacles—economic, linguistic, political, and otherwise—that Chinese scholars had to overcome to obtain research materials from the West. To some extent those difficulties persist.

That many academics in China, some of them quite prominent, were drawn in this general intellectual direction would become more and more evident as Chinese scholars made contact with and sought the assistance of the National Humanities Institute, the small institute then located in Washinton, D.C., whose president is Joseph Baldacchino and whose chairman I am. The website of NHI (www.nhinet.org) makes available much scholarly writing and other research material.

In 1999 I was invited to participate in the triennial meeting of the Chinese Comparative Literature Association in Chengdu in the province of Sichuan. The meeting was called an international symposium, and its theme was cross-cultural communication. The president of the association, Professor Yue Daiyun at Beijing University, asked me to present a paper and to cochair the keynote panel with her. I would eventually learn that Professor Yue is one of China's most famous intellectuals, a public figure, whose influence extends beyond the academic world. She is known for her strong interest in Chinese culture in relation to issues of globalization. Though the Chengdu meeting had an international flavor and was quite large, there were but a handful of participants from Western countries. Unexpectedly, I was asked to make additional presentations. To my astonishment, I, a political scientist from the United States, was asked to offer concluding remarks in the final plenary session about what should be the general direction of research in the era of globalization.

During the same visit to China I was invited to meet scholars at Beijing University and Xinghua University (which may be Beijing University's main competitor for academic preeminence).

That Chinese students of comparative literature and culture would be interested in me, a professor specializing in political philosophy, requires an explanation. I have always had a strong interest in the relationship between politics and culture and have written extensively on the role of the imagination, not least in fiction and poetry, in shaping our outlook on life. My academic work extends more generally to central topics of philosophy, including the epistemology of the humanities, and to the subject of humanism, which is today attracting much attention among Chinese intellectuals. More specifically, I have closely studied and made much use of the ideas of the American thinker Irving Babbitt (1865–1933), a scholar whose interests ranged from literary and cultural to social and political questions. Babbitt was also a pioneer of the discipline of comparative literature. Through his Chinese students at Harvard he had a not insignificant influence in China before communism. Today, as China struggles to define its postcommunist identity, the interest in Babbitt has revived.

The main sponsor of my lecture series at Beijing University was Professor Yue, who, besides having been reelected president of the Chinese Comparative Literature Association, was then director of the university's Institute for Chinese and Comparative Culture. One of my lectures was hosted and introduced by Professor Yan Shao Dang, the head of the department of Chinese.

The lectures were attended by sizeable audiences made up mostly of doctoral and other graduate students and faculty members, some from outside of Beijing University. Though most of the listeners knew at least some English, the lectures were translated paragraph by paragraph, which doubled the time of delivery. I was struck first by the intense and sustained attention of the listeners and then by the incisiveness, liveliness, and outspokenness of the questions and comments offered by members of the audience.

Chinese interest in my work has continued, and other of my writings have been translated and published. In 2002 I was invited to give a plenary address at the triennial meeting of the Chinese Comparative Literature Association in Nanjing. One of China's most respected publishers, San Lian, whose international repertoire is quite wide and growing, recently brought out an anthology intended to convey the intellectual concerns and orientation of the National Humanities Institute and its scholarly journal, *Humanitas,* which Joseph Baldacchino and I coedit. This volume includes an excerpt from Babbitt's *Literature and the American College* (1908) and a number of articles from *Humanitas.* The book's Chinese title, *Humanitas: Rethinking It All,* is taken from the title of an editorial statement in the first issue of the journal (fall 1992/winter 1993) in its current format. That same statement introduces the Chinese book.

As these examples demonstrate, in today's China communist political orthodoxy is a great deal less rigid, influential, and intrusive than it once was. That ideas like mine would be tolerated in China and welcomed among leading scholars is one indication among many that Chinese society is slowly shedding its totalitarian ways. I hasten to add that today's China is a country of great, often disturbing, paradoxes, and that the limited freedoms gained by the Chinese people are still precarious.

My lectures at Beijing University were prepared with a Chinese audience in mind, but their philosophical argument was addressed to anyone who would consider it. I developed a thesis regarding the moral and cultural requirements of peaceful relations among and within societies and cultures centering on the old philosophical issue of universality and particularity. I tried to explain that diverse peoples can meet on common ground and keep the peace without shedding their own distinctiveness.

I have long worked to help rearticulate, revise, and supplement certain old Western traditions. I have done so in part by trying to bring them into fruitful juxtaposition with certain important but neglected and insufficiently understood insights of modernity. The lectures and the book apply the results of these philosophical investigations to questions of globalization and multiculturalism.

My work over the years has made me a dissenter from the ways in which problems of globalization and multiculturalism are most commonly approached in the Western world today. In my view, good relations among diverse cultures, nationalities, and individuals require that moral and cultural nihilism and relativism, as ordinarily understood, be overcome. Though I have criticisms of most traditional notions of universality and am unwilling to adopt the more abstract or amorphous universalism that is fashionable in some circles today, I think it is possible to embrace the notion of universality in reconstituted form. But so is there a need for a substantially revised understanding of particularity. To cultivate personal, national, or cultural distinctiveness need not mean to neglect or undermine universality. On the contrary, particularity is indispensable to universality.

Perhaps my background helps explain my interest in the relation between universality and particularity. I was born and raised in Sweden. I was a doctoral student working on my dissertation at Uppsala University when a desire for greater academic freedom brought me to the United States many years ago. My academic career has been in America, but my ties to my native country and to Europe have remained strong. For many years I have taught at the Catholic University of America, but I am a non-Catholic who grew up in a Protestant country. Though I am a Swede by upbringing and other cultural formation, my scholarship has not been concerned with specifically Swedish subjects. Working out my philosophical ideas, I have been influenced by thinkers of many nationalities, notably Irving Babbitt, an American, and Benedetto Croce, an Italian. Thinkers from other countries, including Germany and England, have affected my outlook. In Sweden I had the good fortune of having the philosopher Folke Leander as a teacher in the gymnasium. Non-Western sources have influenced me as well.

That a native of Sweden who lives in the United States and draws eclectically from American and European thought should be invited to China to lecture on issues related to multiculturalism might seem a prime example of globalization effacing the distinguishing characteristics of cultures, nations, and persons, but this is not how I experienced these events and circumstances. In China I felt my own Westernness, made distinctive by my Swedish origins and my life in America, more acutely than ever. Indeed, my visits to China sharpened my understanding of my own cultural identity. Yet, at the same time, the transpersonal, transcultural life of humanity became more concrete to me than ever. I was strongly aware that my hosts and listeners at Beijing University, including the most "modern" among them, represented an ancient civilization, but I found in that Chinese distinctiveness not merely an obstacle to communication but a challenge to improved understanding of self and humanity. My visits to China and much other contact with Chinese men and women have confirmed, as did my earlier experience of America and Europe, the potential compatibility, indeed union, of universality and particularity. This union is a possibility when cultures meet not so much because differences are blurred but because they are in some ways intensified.

The reception and discussion of the Beijing lectures were for me an emphatic refutation of the doctrine currently fashionable in Western universities that there can be no real meeting of minds and imaginations among representatives of different cultures or even among individuals within the same culture. At the same time, both my lectures and the response to them illustrated that our common humanity cannot be discussed except in the accents of particular individuals and peoples. Deep attachment to a particular historically evolved civilization need not be a hindrance to understanding and appreciating a different civilization. Such allegiance is, on the contrary, a precondition for such comprehension as well as for any more than superficial grasp of the higher humanity of mankind. Genuine understanding and harmony among individuals and peoples involve the dialectic coexistence, the synthesis, of particularity and universality.

Acknowledgments

While preparing this book I incurred some debts that I would especially like to acknowledge. My friend Joseph Baldacchino, with whom I share the editorship of *Humanitas* and the leadership of the National Humanities Institute, is my frequent partner in conversation, and I always benefit from his thoughtful comments. This volume is a revised and expanded version of a book published by Beijing University Press that originated as a lecture series at Beijing University. Randall Auxier, the editor of the Library of Living Philosophers at Southern Illinois University, who is a refreshingly free but also philosophically disciplined spirit, gave me suggestions for how I might revise the book for this English edition. Even when I did not follow his recommendations I was intellectually stimulated by them. Laurence Reardon, a doctoral student of mine, compiled the index and offered other valuable assistance. The book also gained substantially from the editorial process at the University of Missouri Press.

Finally, I want to express my deep gratitude to my wife, Marianne, who has been willing over the years to put up with my long hours in my study.

A COMMON
HUMAN
GROUND

Introduction

Work on the lectures from which this book originated started about two years before the atrocities of September 11, 2001. The first paragraph of chapter 1, for example, which formulates the global social and political context for the philosophical investigations to be undertaken, introduced the lectures in Beijing as well as the Chinese book based on them (see the preface). The events of September 11 have merely given gruesome evidence of the practical import of the issues that are addressed in these pages and lent urgency to a crucial question: Could tensions among peoples, societies, and cultures be lessened? This book is a response to that question. How we think about the question and how we handle it in practice will decide the future of the world. In this area, illusions or carelessness could have devastating consequences. This is one reason why any serious thinker will approach the subject with some trepidation as well as a sense of inadequacy.

Contrary to postmodernist intellectual trends, this book affirms the existence, both actual and potential, of a shared, unifying humanity, but it simultaneously affirms the great value of diversity.

Especially in this era of globalization it is important to nourish and protect what is properly distinctive to individuals, peoples, and cultures. To do so is fully compatible with cultivating a common humanity. In fact, the two can be shown to be different aspects of the same humanizing effort. Here we come to the core of the thesis of this book, which will undoubtedly, at least initially, evoke incredulity in many quarters: *Unique particularity is potentially a manifestation of universality itself,* a source of its richness, strength, and adaptability. What will strike many as nothing less than a contradiction in terms is a living human reality. This thesis has direct and wide-ranging implications for how we think and behave as individuals and societies, domestically and internationally.

The seemingly paradoxical thesis of the book is that in an important sense the truly common human ground is discovered *through* the differences among individuals and peoples. Our humanity is stimulated and deepened by the challenge of diversity. In a world of moral, aesthetic, and intellectual homogeneity, our humanity would shrivel.

Given the scope and complexity of the philosophical issues to be explored, it may be helpful to provide a general idea of the structure of the argument. A summary of this kind may facilitate the absorption of particular points along the way. The book develops a new approach to the problem of universality and particularity, with special emphasis on how it relates to unity and diversity among individuals, groups, and peoples. Chapter 1 defines the central issue and connects it with the problem of alleviating conflict. This chapter and the one following it propose "humanism" as a convenient term for a heightened awareness of the intimate relation between universality and particularity. Chapter 2 goes more deeply into the moral and cultural dimensions of relations among individuals, societies, and cultures and into the tie between these dimensions of life and the requirements of peace. The chapter considers some relevant traditional Western views and a few modern challenges to them. Chapter 3 argues that appreciation of the merits of other cultures requires first a deep allegiance to a particular culture. It proposes what it calls cosmopolitan humanism as essential to achieving greater respect among societies. Chapter 4 emphasizes that history is a powerful force in the present and that human existence is inescapably historical. The chapter shows that history is a guide to universality but that its lessons must be creatively applied to new circumstances. Chapter 5 explores further the ethical aspect of the common life of mankind. It argues for cosmopolitan breadth and flexibility in how ethical universality is understood. Chapters 6 and 7 deal with the failure to recognize the historicity of human existence and how that failure leads to the adoption of a purely abstract notion of universality and a related disdain for particularity. The desire in some quarters for a homogeneous global moral regime is shown to represent a serious and dangerous misunderstanding of universality. The remaining chapters explain in greater depth the needed alternative to either postmodernist nihilism or abstract universalism. Here, as earlier, the book's philosophical approach is referred to as "value-centered historicism," a term that the author has used in previous writing. The crux of this way of thinking is recognizing the historical, dialectical, living character of human existence and, most especially, the possibility of synthesis of particularity and universality. These concluding chapters criticize what the book terms the *idiosyncratic society* and argue for what it calls the *versatile society*. These chapters give final form to the idea that whenever the values of goodness, truth, or beauty are realized, universality and particularity are mutually implicated in, and greatly in need of, each other. The book ends by exploring uniqueness as potentially the highest manifestation of universality and by discussing what this notion means for how individuals, peoples, and civilizations might meet on a common human ground.

One way to make a philosophical position clear is to contrast it with what it is not. This book makes its case partly by criticizing deficient approaches to the problem of universality and particularity. The views of which the book is critical and which form a foil for its own argument tend to fall into one of three broad categories. One is the multiculturalism and postmodernism that flatly dismisses universality, or "foundationalism," in every form. Many writers, including Richard Rorty and Stanley Fish, have contributed to this kind of thinking. Another point of view that is found unacceptable here is abstract universalism, which sees history and particularity as such as meaningless and even degrading. Though Plato's philosophy has another side, he gave this strain of thought a powerful push. Today those who assert a universality separate from history include Leo Strauss and his followers, who berate what they call "historical relativism" or "historicism." The third general category of ideas that is deemed deficient in this book is sometimes linked to the second. It is a kind of traditionalism, an ahistorical conception of history, as it were, that tends to lose universality in rigidity and formalism. Most often this orientation is little more than a general unwillingness to change with the times, but there are also philosophical traditionalists, including S. H. Nasr and Tage Lindbom, who see Truth as having been deposited in a particular tradition. The latter should not be adjusted to circumstance but must be protected against change.

It is understood, of course, that broad categories of this type ignore philosophical nuances and qualifications and often significant differences among individual thinkers, but, for the most part, the criticisms made here are aimed less at individuals than at broad general trends. The book's argument does not depend on getting each mentioned thinker just right.

What follows is a large argument with broad implications that is set forth rather concisely, and it deliberately avoids in-depth discussion of some issues. The author has dealt elsewhere with aspects of most of the philosophical questions discussed in this book, and many points made here receive more support in those writings. A reader of the manuscript for this book pointed out that people unfamiliar with the author's other work might think that he was ignoring or glossing over some philosophical problems and insisted that the author overcome any reluctance to cite his own previous publications. It may be optimistic to hope that the resulting number of such references in the footnotes will not strike the reader as unseemly.

CHAPTER ONE

Peace as the Union of
Universality and Particularity

Probably the greatest challenge facing mankind in the twenty-first century is the danger of conflict between peoples and cultures. There is an urgent need to explore in depth possibilities for minimizing tensions and to undertake efforts to reduce them. Horrendous consequences can result from superficiality, carelessness, and naïveté in defining the dangers and from delay in trying to lessen them. Yet the all-too-human desire to avoid painful self-scrutiny and reorientation of action makes human beings indulge a seemingly unlimited capacity for wishful thinking. Many in the West and elsewhere trust in scientific progress and general enlightenment to reduce the danger of conflict, but we need only look to the century preceding this one—the most murderous and inhumane in the history of mankind—to recognize that the spread of science and allegedly sophisticated modern ideas does not reduce the self-absorption or belligerence of human beings. It only provides them with new means of asserting their will. Others in the West trust in political and economic schemes to alleviate tensions, "democracy" and "free markets" being the two most popular at the moment. These prescriptions for how to promote good relations between peoples give short shrift to a subject that may in fact be far more important, one that requires greater depth and subtlety of mind and that is also not fashionable: the moral and cultural preconditions of peace. Whatever the importance of other factors, attempts to avoid conflict among peoples and individuals are not likely to be successful without a certain quality of human will and imagination. That this subject is receiving so much less attention than proposals for introducing technology and manipulating political and economic institutions is a sign that our societies are not now well equipped to deal with the most pressing problem of the new century.

We may state the question before us in the language of multiculturalism: Will it be possible for culturally diverse peoples and individuals to live peacefully together? Cultural diversity there has always been, but today new forms of communication and greater opportunities of migration are bringing people of very different backgrounds into closer and more frequent contact. This shrinking of the world has given great urgency to finding sources of accommodation, harmony, and tolerance. What are the possible grounds upon which diverse peoples and individuals might coexist in some harmony? That topic will be investigated here, with emphasis on the moral and cultural dimension of the question.

Those who dominate the debate on multiculturalism in the West have little or no interest in considering whether human experience might contain moral or aesthetical elements that transcend the distinctiveness of particular groups and societies and that might constitute a bond of shared humanity. These intellectuals simply deny the existence of universality. They espouse either the typical modern "liberal" view that all values are ultimately subjective and relative or the more radical form of antiuniversalism that is postmodernist "historicism." For these people, peaceful relations among peoples and individuals could stem only from tolerance and clever management of differences, not from a common core of humanity.

To address the central issue we must establish a wider philosophical and historical context than the one provided by the current debate about multiculturalism. A broader exposure to what lies within the human range gives us not only more examples of the diversity of mankind but indications of substantial transhistorical and transcultural commonalities. Attending to a greater body of evidence than is typically done today reveals persistent moral and cultural patterns suggestive of a unity of human experience. Certain attitudes and forms of life found in different parts of the globe bespeak the existence of a more than subjective and time-bound apprehension of the self and the world. Discernible amidst the diversity of human tastes and preferences is a fundamental confluence of moral and aesthetical sensibility. This confluence is visible not only in mankind's strictly religious traditions but in the moral and cultural life more generally. There have been recurring and systematic efforts over the centuries and across cultural boundaries to constrain the least-admirable traits of humanity and to promote a higher potential of life, to foster characteristics seen as being the best and noblest as well as a source of social cohesion and happiness. As a label for the endeavor to cultivate what is highest in man we might adopt the old word *humanism*. Since that word has no single definition, the following discussion will have to make clearer how it is used here.

Whether or in what sense multicultural diversity can be tempered and harmonized by a genuinely common human element depends on the answer to a fundamental question that has occupied and divided philosophers down the centuries. The question concerns the relationship between universality and particularity, the two pervasive elements of experience that in their apparent coexistence and tension constitute human life. Many terms have been used to refer to different aspects of the paradox of existence: unity and diversity, rest and motion, order and disorder, permanence and impermanence, harmony and disharmony, sameness and otherness—to name a few.

Although in direct, concrete experience the two dimensions are inseparable, philosophers have been prone to discount the ultimate significance of the one dimension and attribute reality only to the other. This was the case with Plato, as he is usually read, who posited a transcendent sphere of changeless forms, extolling a One opposed to all diversity and movement. For Plato, individual phenomena, the Many, were a part of the flux and had no meaning of their own; man should try as far as possible to escape from whatever is particular and changing to what is universal and unchanging. Universality—whose different forms were the good, the true, and the beautiful—was ahistorical and was threatened and obscured by the historical flux. Today, at the other extreme, postmodernists, represented in America by Richard Rorty, deny the existence of enduring standards of goodness, truth, and beauty. They recognize only historical particularity, contingency, and subjectivity, the element of existence that Plato associated with meaninglessness. Rejecting the notion of higher order or meaning, postmodernists celebrate diversity and advocate tolerance for differences among individuals and groups. They recognize no common human core.

These contrasting ways of thinking exemplify what Irving Babbitt (1865–1933), the American literary scholar and cultural thinker, calls "metaphysics of the One" and "metaphysics of the Many." The two philosophical orientations discount, disparage, or disregard one of the dimensions of life, either the One or the Many. They are both "metaphysical" in the sense that they are not content to base their view of reality on the facts of immediate experience but are selective in considering the evidence. Each of the two orientations distorts even the element that most attracts its interest, for it attributes to that element a univocal character that life itself does not give. Babbitt's view is that "life does not give here an element of oneness and there an element of change. It gives a *oneness that is always changing.* The oneness and the change are inseparable."[1]

How we regard the relationship between universality and particularity directly affects how we think about humanism and multiculturalism. Stark consequences result from assuming that universality and particularity have little or nothing in common or that one or the other does not really exist. If humanism is a moral and cultural proclivity to respect and promote the higher potential of particular human beings, then it would seem to be badly served by a philosophy that belittles particularity and attaches no importance to human individuality as such. If, as in Platonic philosophy, only pure universality has value, distinctive traits of personality are of no interest, are even detrimental to the higher life. The standard for elevating existence is a changeless,

---

1. Irving Babbitt, *Rousseau and Romanticism* (New York: Houghton Mifflin, 1919; with a new introduction by Claes G. Ryn, New Brunswick: Transaction Publishers, 1991), lxxiii (emphasis in original). Babbitt was professor of French and comparative literature at Harvard. His other books include *Democracy and Leadership* (1924) and *Literature and the American College* (1908). He was the founder and chief advocate of what has been called American Humanism or the New Humanism. A scholar-sage with a deep interest in Eastern thought, Babbitt strongly influenced many Asian students, some of whom became prominent in their own countries. Chinese students of his contributed to the periodical *Xueheng* (*Critical Review*). The movement they started is today receiving new interest.

unitary norm above all individuality, and man's purpose is to imitate it. Freedom and diversity introduce distractions, complications that should be limited and minimized. What is needed is not room for improvisation but conformity to the preexisting norm. Humanism framed on such a basis, if indeed it can be called humanism at all, detaches itself from concrete, historical life. It becomes strongly disinclined to accommodate human individuality. To people who see potential value in personal uniqueness as such and in the sometimes unexpected opportunities of life, this kind of universalistic humanism must appear cold, inflexible, unimaginative, or distant. In the West, universalism of this kind comes in many forms, including Jacobin rights of man, neo-Thomist moral rationalism, and ahistorical natural right thinking of the type advocated by Leo Strauss. Among religious thinkers who emphasize the vast distance between the concrete, immanent world and the divine ground of being are the theologian Karl Barth, with his notion of God as "wholly other," and the intellectual historian Eric Voegelin, with his Platonic notion of radical transcendence.

Postmodernist multiculturalism, in contrast, calls attention to the pervasiveness and inevitability of diversity. Since it does not recognize universality, it must resign itself to the impossibility of any real harmony between human beings. Even individuals from the same cultural group are, though superficially alike and connected, separated by personal background and therefore ultimately isolated and alone. Multiculturalism of this kind drowns in a welter of differences and change, incapable of distinguishing between fruitful and destructive diversity, between legitimate and illegitimate self-assertion, between personal creativity and mere idiosyncrasy. Within this outlook, the word *humanism* is ultimately meaningless, as is the word *culture*. Because it rejects every notion of universality, postmodernist multiculturalism excludes the possibility of a more than superficial and transitory sense of common purpose and togetherness. It can offer no robust and lasting counterweight to social dissolution or arbitrary power.

But these two extreme positions, ahistorical universalism and "historicist" particularism, do not exhaust the possibilities in thinking about the relationship between universality and particularity. Differently understood, universality and particularity need not be incongruous. They can be shown to be in a sense intimately related, even mutually dependent. In the light of this understanding of universality and particularity, humanism and multiculturalism are seen to be not only compatible but to be different aspects of one and the same effort to realize life's higher potential. Diversity need not be a threat to unity; it can, as unified by humanistic discipline, enrich and enhance the common. This idea has vast implications—not merely for scholars concerned about philosophical precision. Philosophy at its best is about concrete life and exists for the sake of life. That universality and particularity might be reconciled, and with them humanism and multiculturalism, has far-reaching practical significance. On the possibility of such reconciliation may rest the hope for averting conflict among societies and cultures in the twenty-first century. The possibility of synthesis between particularity and universality bespeaks a potential for creative rapprochement among diverse individuals, societies, and cultures—not at the expense of their diversity but rather *through* their diversity.

Establishing that universality and particularity may exist in union as well as in tension will require an extended discussion of difficult questions. Clarifying how they are related is here not an end in itself but intended to advance the overarching purpose of assessing whether in our shrinking world it may be possible for diverse nations and groups to have peaceful, indeed, morally and culturally enriching, relations. Keeping that purpose in mind will protect us from an overly technical approach to the fundamental philosophical issue.

CHAPTER TWO

Moral and Cultural
Preconditions of Harmony

No serious examination of the questions of peace and creative rapprochement can avoid their moral dimension. The fact that political, economic, and other social circumstances strongly influence human behavior does not excuse us from considering the character of individuals as a source of conduct. To understand the origins of the sort of conduct that reduces rather than increases the danger of conflict and understand how society might assist in fostering such behavior we must examine man's basic moral predicament. Our frame of reference in trying to determine the terms of moral existence will be the evidence offered by our own experience, as augmented and elucidated by the historical experience of mankind.

By attending to the moral requirements of peace we shall, at the same time, advance the discussion of universality and particularity. In its most fundamental aspect, universality is a moral force, a force on which even truth and beauty ultimately depend because they cannot in the end do without the centering of the personality made possible by moral will. Universality in general can be seen as the power that orders the diversity of groups, individuals, and desires so as to make them part of the higher human life. Though radically incompatible with some manifestations of particularity, universality is potentially consonant with other manifestations. It can blend with and shape diversity, making diversity the medium for its own higher unity. Universality brings concrete and specific good into the world by embodying itself in particularity, giving such particularity a special dignity, raising it above inchoate individuality, and forming the antithesis of individuality organized for evil purposes. Humanism may in this context be broadly defined as the deliberate effort to understand and foster that higher development. Its task is to balance and harmonize unity and diversity and thereby to enrich the personal and the common life.

Many people in the West, and perhaps especially in the United States, rely on facile prescriptions for how to keep a multicultural mankind at peace. These prescriptions include closer economic ties, more technocratic enlightenment, more liberal tolerance, more international institutions, more free markets, and more democracy. Sometimes proponents of these measures exhibit a sentimental and naive "brotherhood of man" and assume that despite the differences among peoples and individuals all human beings are, deep down, the same and really only waiting to embrace. Not all of the mentioned formulas lack utility, and they are advanced with varying degrees of naïveté or realism, but, as ordinarily presented, they avoid what may be the very heart of the problem. They do not, except in a cursory manner, raise the moral and cultural preconditions of peace. They do not provide what seems most needed: a sturdy check on the human propensity to dominate and exploit others and a well-grounded respect for the attainments and legitimate claims of others.

Nationalistic arrogance and economic ruthlessness endanger international harmony in a direct, palpable manner. But these are only particularly troublesome instances of a more general threat to good relations among cultures, namely that, instead of interacting on the level of what is morally, aesthetically, and intellectually noblest in each, cultures encounter each other on the level of the mercenary, the grasping, the crude, the vulgar, and the shoddy. Whatever momentary benefits may be derived from such interaction, it does not form a basis for peace. Much of the popular Western culture that is absorbed by non-Western societies today creates a superficial commonality across borders, but it does not elicit among discerning elites the respect that might forge ties of lasting friendship. Cultures coming into closer contact while displaying their least-admirable traits may in time recoil from each other, a reaction that is bound to be exploited by opportunists on all sides, who are looking for excuses to exercise their will to power.

Here we must face the central problem that all societies and all persons are torn between their own higher and lower potentialities. This view of human nature is common to a large number of traditional philosophies, ethical systems, and religions, ranging from ancient Greek and Roman philosophy and Christianity to Sufi philosophy, Hinduism, Confucianism, Buddhism, and Islam. The obstacles to realizing the values of goodness, truth, and beauty and to achieving peaceful relations among individuals and groups are ubiquitous. Historical and social circumstances may aggravate the problem, but its most fundamental cause is that human beings tend to shrink from the necessary effort, prone as they are to less-commendable desires. Progress requires protracted exertions. To the extent that a people falls short of what is best in its own culture, its members will exhibit such examples of self-indulgence as greed and intolerance. This will not only threaten its own social cohesion, but will also inevitably undermine international harmony.

The view of human nature and society just alluded to was until the last century or two wholly dominant in the Western world. It is similar to beliefs long influential in the East. A central feature of the traditional Western understanding of the human condition is the mentioned belief that human nature is in constant tension between desires that will enhance and complete existence and ones that, though they may bring short-term satisfaction, are destructive of a deeper harmony of life. To realize the higher meaning of life—what the Greeks called *eudaimonia* (happiness)—the individual needs to discipline his appetites of the moment, even try to extinguish some of them, with a view to his own enduring good. By happiness was meant not a collection of pleasures, but a special sense of well-being and self-respect that comes from living responsibly and nobly, as befits a truly human being. The person aspiring to that kind of life must frequently say no to pleasures and advantages of the moment, namely those that are inimical to a more deeply satisfying existence. Once attained, the life of happiness is its own reward. Aristotle emphasized the need for acquiring early in life the kind of habits that will enable the person to resist destructive desires and develop the soundness of character that orients the personality toward happiness. To grow as a human being the individual must live in association with others. A good society will supply the varied needs of a safe and comfortable existence, but most important, it will help civilize and humanize the person. Though family, groups, and social institutions can assist the person in achieving a happy life, no amount of external guidance or encouragement can substitute for individual effort.

The good life has many aspects and prerequisites—economic, political, intellectual, aesthetical, and moral—but there was widespread agreement in old Western society, whether predominantly Greek, Roman, or Christian, that the orientation of character, specifically, the quality of a person's will, is crucial to realizing life's higher potential. A person who lacks the moral strength required for right conduct cannot secure happiness by dint of intellectual brilliance, imaginative power, or economic productivity. Christianity has regarded man's cleft will, his often desiring what is contrary to his own higher good, as the crux of human life. Though the individual should always strive to contain his selfish and shortsighted inclinations and try to act responsibly, his human weakness makes him heavily dependent on God. Protestant Christianity has been especially concerned to emphasize that even the best of men are unable to overcome their sinful inclinations on their own and need to be rescued by divine grace.

Western tradition, then, has, for the most part, regarded moral character and the performance of good actions as the primary measure of human goodness. The moral and religious wisdom of the West has explained and encouraged the kind of working on self that in time will build real meaning and worth into human existence. Whether the aim has been achieving the happiness and nobility of a worldly, civilized life of the type that Aristotle advocates, or achieving the special peace of otherworldliness and saintliness that Christianity regards as the very culmination of the religious life, there is no substitute for protracted, sometimes difficult moral striving. "I am the way and the life and the truth," proclaimed Jesus of Nazareth. Christianity has assumed that the validity of this claim could be confirmed only by one willing to undertake the kind of actions entailed by that statement. Protestant Christianity puts particular stress on the need for faith, but all of Christianity agrees that true faith shows itself in action. The East offers many examples of a very similar outlook. In Buddhism, especially that of the Hinayana variety, the right Way is the diligent working on or against self to extinguish needless worldly desire. In *The Dhammapada,* the holy text attributed, at least in its general spirit, to the Buddha, we find these words about the path to Nirvana: "You yourself must make an effort."[1] Through acts of will, man's lower self is transcended.

In the West, perhaps the most radical and influential challenge to this view of human nature has been that of Jean-Jacques Rousseau (1712–1778). Rousseau was, among other things, the main intellectual inspiration for the French Jacobins, who spearheaded the French Revolution. Rousseau considers the view of human nature just described to be profoundly mistaken. Contrary to Christianity, he sees in man no lower inclinations, no original sin. Man is born good, and his nature remains good. Man as he once existed in his primitive state, before the appearance of society, was a pure, simple, peaceful, happy creature. Such evil as exists in the world is due not to some perversity in man, but to wrongly constructed social norms and institutions. Destroy the bad society, Rousseau contends, and man's goodness will flow.

The view of Rousseau and related thinkers represents nothing less than a revolution in the understanding of morality and social existence. To summarize the change, virtue ceases to be an attribute of character and right willing and becomes instead an attribute of feeling and imagination, a matter of the "heart." The old measure of goodness was responsible individual action. The new measure of goodness is tearful empathy—"pity." No longer is moral virtue thought to result from sometimes discomforting self-scrutiny and a diligent working on self. Since man is by nature good, there is no need for him to guard against his own lower impulses of the moment or to undertake a difficult disciplining of self. Neither is there any need for civilized norms or for social groups and institutions to buttress morality. Liberate man from traditional constraints, and goodness will flow spontaneously from human nature. A brotherhood of man will reconstitute society. In the concluding paragraph of his *First Discourse,* Rousseau sums up

---

1. *The Dhammapada,* trans. with an essay by Irving Babbitt (New York: New Directions Publishing, 1965), 43.

the superiority of the new virtue over the old. "O virtue!" he exclaims in praise of the sentimental morality he professes, "are so many difficulties and so much preparation necessary in order to know you? Are your principles not engraved in all hearts?" Having declared man good, Rousseau and his followers transfer the most significant struggle of human existence from the inner life of the person to society, where evil forces must be defeated by the virtuous to make a good society possible. Rousseau's redefinition of morality had a profound influence in the Western world, where it soon began to invade even the Christian churches. That Rousseauism should have become so popular is hardly surprising. It is after all rather flattering to be told that there is no evil in yourself and perhaps even more gratifying to learn that it is not you but society that must change for the better. Rousseau not only absolves the individual of blame; he attributes to him nobility and goodness. Rousseau's contemporary in England, the political thinker and statesman Edmund Burke (1729–1797), says of Rousseau that he advocates an "ethics of vanity."[2]

But the traditional view of human nature and society has been undermined also by another powerful force, the kind of rationalism that seized the initiative in the West with the Enlightenment. Representatives of that broad intellectual movement have rejected the older view of man as unscientific. Their conception of reason is heavily slanted in the direction of natural science methodology and has little room for what might be called humane wisdom. A better life, they argue, depends on man's applying science and rationality, as they define them, to the problems of life. Improving human existence is a matter of restructuring society in accordance with scientific insights. The issue of moral character as traditionally defined seems to the Enlightenment rationalists marginal or irrelevant.

Rousseauistic sentimental virtue and Enlightenment rationalism might seem to represent entirely different approaches to life, but they share elements that have made them frequent allies, both theoretically

2. Jean-Jacques Rousseau, *The Basic Political Writings, First Discourse,* trans. Donald Cress (Indianapolis: Hackett Publishing, 1987), 21; Edmund Burke, *Letter to a Member of the National Assembly* (1791), in *The Works of the Rt. Hon. Edmund Burke* (Boston: Little, Brown & Company, 1865–1867).

and practically, in the modern Western world and beyond. Especially important in our present context is that both movements reject the old view that goodness in individuals and society is the result of the inner struggle and striving of persons. The one movement rejects this view because it believes it has discovered a good, previously suppressed human nature; the other does so because it regards the old view of human nature as unscientific. Both movements abandon the idea of the morally divided self and belittle the need for moral self-discipline. According to them, selfishness, ruthlessness, avarice, and conflict are not due to any chronic weakness of humanity to be moderated by self-restraint, but can be overcome by intelligently remaking the social and political exterior. The one movement trusts in the natural goodness of man to set society right; the other trusts in reason and science to show mankind the way to a better world. In current Western academic discussion the word *modernity* typically refers to the mode of rationality and science that became dominant with the Enlightenment, but if it is true that this kind of rationalism has put a deep imprint on the modern Western mind, it is also true that Rousseauistic romanticism and related cultural currents have had a profound influence on the moral sensibility and imagination of Western man. One of the many examples of the two impulses coexisting and cooperating is social engineering. The advocates of comprehensive social planning aim to reconstruct society according to an allegedly scientific blueprint, but they derive their moral sanction and inspiration from the new sentimental virtue. While the ethic of pity and benevolence defines the end, "rational" manipulation provides the means. In the cultural life of the West as well as in other parts of the world, the coexistence of technology and sentimentality is everywhere, as when romantic emotion of various types is transmitted by such means as television, radio, the Internet, VCRs, computers, and CDs.

Though the older Western view of human nature and society has not disappeared, it has lost much of its influence. It has been diluted or otherwise changed, notably by the influences just described. Often the West of today presents an odd mixture of diverse, poorly integrated elements. An important question when considering the prospect for international peace is whether the more traditional Western view can reemerge in a form that incorporates the best of modernity while shedding old doctrinal encrustations.

So momentous are the mentioned issues and so far-reaching are their implications that the slightest propensity for wishful thinking in addressing them can have grave consequences. It is necessary to ask whether there is a connection between the fact that sentimental morality and Enlightenment rationality made such great advances in the West and elsewhere in the nineteenth and twentieth centuries and the fact that the century just past saw wars and mass killings of a previously unseen scope. These horrors have in any case cast grave doubt on the belief in human goodness and in the ability of science to create a better world. One has to wonder if these man-made disasters were not in large part due to the slipping of traditional moral restraints.

Postmodernism has produced a partial critique of the intellectual currents of the last two centuries, focusing on the rigidities and arbitrary assumptions of rationalism and positivism and on the more or less subtle grasp for power that they entail. At the same time, postmodernism is in important respects a part of modernity in a broader sense. Its indiscriminate opposition to structures and inhibitions shows it to be in large measure a return to and extension of Rousseauistic romanticism. Like Rousseauism, postmodernism sets aside the question of moral self-restraint that more traditional Western thought deemed all-important.

This discussion of the moral terms of human existence, which has been based largely on Western ideas and circumstances, permits no firm conclusion, but it has brought out moral and cultural issues that must be given great weight when exploring the possibility of unity in diversity. The complexity and subtlety of these issues are obvious even without considering specifically Eastern ways of approaching them that merit attention, especially in this era of globalization. The purpose of the just-completed review has been to demonstrate that human history contains a large body of evidence supporting a view of human nature and society that receives little attention from intellectuals today. It is not philosophically respectable simply to assume the validity of notions of human nature and society that happen to be fashionable at the moment. The philosophical mind is acutely aware of the danger of historical and geographical provincialism, the danger of being confined to the perspectives of the here and now. Philosophy proper wants to weigh *all* the available evidence. It is ready to absorb new insight and to revise or discard old assumptions, but it never excludes ideas from consideration in order to protect intellectual fashion or an accustomed way of life.

CHAPTER THREE

A Cosmopolitan Basis for Peace

The previous chapters have indicated that peaceful relations within a society require moral and cultural effort on the part of the individuals composing it. Edmund Burke expresses the same point of view with regard to the preconditions of freedom. He suggests that both the proper amount of government and the proper amount of liberty will depend on the moral and cultural condition of a people:

> Men are qualified for civil liberty in exact proportion to their disposition to put moral chains upon their own appetites; in proportion as their love of justice is above their rapacity; in proportion as their soundness and sobriety of understanding is above their vanity and presumption; in proportion as they are more disposed to listen to the counsels of the wise and good, in preference to the flattery of knaves. Society cannot exist unless a controlling power upon will and appetite be placed somewhere, and the less of it there is within, the more there must be without. It is ordained in the eternal constitution of things, that men of intemperate minds cannot be free. Their passions forge their fetters.[1]

Burke's argument can be applied to the possibilities of peace. The greater the ability of the members of a society to restrain passions that can cause conflict with others, the less the need for government to impose peace upon them. In the international arena, the chances for peaceful relations are similarly improved to the extent that states are prone to self-restraint. A lack of that same quality increases the danger

---

1. Burke, *Letter to a Member of the National Assembly.*

of conflict. Internationally, conflict sometimes cannot be resolved except by war.

From these observations there emerges a thesis regarding the most basic requirement for harmonizing the diversity of individuals, peoples, and nations: To be conducive to good relations in the long run, political, economic, scientific, and other contacts need to be informed and shaped by a morality of self-control and by corresponding cultural discipline and sensibility. The enlightened self-interest upon which many pin their hopes for peace is itself unconsciously dependent for its sense of direction upon another, more truly common human ground. But if this view is correct, those who now dominate discussions of how to avoid conflict are virtually neglecting the most basic demands of harmonious relations, trusting as they do in political and economic methods that by themselves have limited efficacy and that may in some circumstances even undermine good relations. The Western world has not entirely shed its older moral and cultural assumptions and habits; human patterns built up over many centuries fade only slowly. But in the West at present there are no sustained and systematic efforts to recover and renew the older understanding of man's moral predicament.

What the world seems to need most is a cosmopolitanism that simultaneously affirms cultural uniqueness and pancultural unity and that does so on the basis of complete moral realism. This ethos would be much different from the kind of ecumenism that seeks to promote harmony by having different societies erase whatever is distinctive in favor of homogeneity. A humanistic cosmopolitanism would, on the contrary, encourage particular peoples to be themselves in the sense of living up to their own highest standards. Sound cosmopolitanism must itself be derived from what is most exemplary about the culture that most immediately nourishes it. For a vivid and concrete sense of the good, the true, and the beautiful to be possible, that sense must be deeply rooted in the soil of a particular culture and be alive with the best that this culture has wrought. Only on the basis of intimate familiarity with the highest achievements of one's own society is it possible to have a more than shallow appreciation for the corresponding highest achievements of other societies. How could a person from the West who is ignorant of Aristotle hope to understand Confucius? How could a person from the East who is ignorant of Buddha hope to understand Jesus of Nazareth? To be steeped in one's own traditions is a prerequisite for having deep loyalties but also for having broad sympathies. Only to the superficial observer does a strong attachment to what is culturally distinctive have to undermine a broader unity. Absorbing what is most elevating about one's own society actually prepares and predisposes the individual to recognizing what is admirable about other people's. The humanistic effort increases the awareness of a transcultural human ground, letting individuals from different backgrounds see each other as engaged in a partly common human enterprise, common though of necessity adjusted to the needs and circumstances of time and place.

No individual, however learned and well traveled, can truly master several cultures. A genuine humanism must grow primarily in a particular cultural soil. But humanism is never closed in upon a single heritage. Genuine humanism is, by its very nature, an opening-up of the human personality to the rich possibilities of the higher life. It wishes to know as much as it can of the values that may enhance existence. That an element of cosmopolitanism is integral to humanism does not make it rootless and free-floating, for a real cosmopolitan is strongly attached to his own primary culture. Still, such a person can to some extent feel at home in those other societies in whose higher aspirations he recognizes the better efforts of his own society. The cosmopolitanism that forms part of humanism can be said to be its multicultural dimension. Humanism is attracted to diversity, though not in an indiscriminate manner. It sees in cultural diversity a possible source for a fuller awareness of the universal. Through its special form of multiculturalism, humanism expands and enriches its sense of the manifold potentialities of goodness, truth, and beauty as well as its sense of the deeper unity of human experience. To recognize that the spirit of the higher life transcends individual cultural identities at the very same time that it animates them is to become aware that to live in the particular may be to live in the universal.

It must be noted here that all of human life is for good or ill and that often cultural diversity is not a power for good. It can manifest narrow-

minded provincialism, egotistical partisanship, decadence, recklessness, and brutality and thus be a cause of degradation and conflict.
Variety that is not humanized by concern for the higher life but that
expresses mere arbitrary willfulness or eccentricity can cause great
volatility and worse. Nationalistic self-absorption and arrogance have
been great and frequent sources of trouble for mankind in the last two
centuries. The great trouble with what is ordinarily called multiculturalism today is that it is quite unable to distinguish between diversity
that ennobles and diversity that degrades human life. Postmodernists
reject the distinction between good and evil, high and low. Like Rorty,
many of them reject "seriousness" and advocate a merely "playful"
experimentation as the proper approach to life.[2] They might consider
that children are taught not to play with matches.

It is for the sake of peace, but also for the sake of a more rewarding life for all, that different societies need to cultivate a common
ground in regard to what is most humane in each culture. Here a
heavy responsibility rests on those who set the tone for the longer
run in each society: leaders in philosophy, the arts, religion, politics,
business, and so on. By shaping the will, the mind, and the imagination
of a people, these elites shape the future. It should be clear from the
argument presented here that the proposed humanizing discipline is
very different from trying to replace particularity with an amorphous
abstract or sentimental universalism.

The view being propounded here may be called *cosmopolitan humanism*. This humanism recognizes that distinctive, historically formed
cultural identities can manifest one and the same effort—more or less
successful in particular cases—to achieve a truly satisfying existence.
Representatives of different cultures can reach each other as fellow
human beings *through* their cultural individuality, as shaped by shared
striving. Because the peoples of the world face vastly different circumstances and opportunities, goodness, truth, and beauty can have
meaning and practical efficacy only as incarnated in a myriad of *different*
ways. Moral and other customs must differ in specifics according to

2. Richard Rorty, *Consequences of Pragmatism: Essays, 1972–1980* (Minneapolis:
University of Minnesota Press, 1982), 87–88.

time and place, but the variety can be the diversification of a single universal purpose beyond personal inclination and convenience. Manners and decorum vary from culture to culture, but in their highest aim they manifest the same recognition that human beings should act with dignity, elegance, and courtesy. Art comes in many forms and styles, but each expresses a common desire that life be enhanced through artistic vision, beauty, and refinement. *Through* all the diversity, not in spite of it, there emerges a transcultural awareness that life is potentially full of meaning and worth and must not be frittered away or permitted to turn barbarous.

Universality shows itself in the world, then, not by drawing attention away from or by abolishing the particular, but by particularizing itself. To be part of human experience at all, universality must acquire concrete shape. It must become known in the particular person, the particular action, the particular poem, the particular idea. It does not belong to a transcendent sphere lacking all concreteness; such a sphere would be empty and without human interest. In so far as a culture's finest achievements embody universality, they can speak also to representatives of other cultures, although absorbing them may sometimes require great effort.

A humanist may deeply respect ways and beliefs long admired by his own culture, because he senses that, at their best, they embody the spirit of an intrinsically good and rewarding life. Yet a person wishing to be humane must guard against one-sidedness, provincialism, blindness, and rigidity. Convention and routine can become stale and begin to stifle the moral and cultural effort that is man's connection with universality. For that connection to remain strong and vibrant, tradition needs to be continually challenged, refreshed, and developed. Although indebted to the traditions of a certain society for its sense of direction, humanism tries to base its judgments of goodness, truth, and beauty on direct intuition rather than on inherited opinion.[3] It is acutely aware of the complexity and changeability of human existence

---

3. For an extensive discussion of the role of intuition in seeing life afresh, see Claes G. Ryn, *Will, Imagination and Reason: Babbitt, Croce and the Problem of Reality*, 2d enl. ed. (Chicago: Regnery Books, 1986; with a new introduction by the author, New Brunswick: Transaction Publishers, 1997).

and of the inevitability of disagreement, even among persons of noble motive, about how life should best be lived. Historical circumstances may sharpen and refine the sensibilities of one society or individual in certain respects and dull and warp the sensibilities of another. The variety of approaches to the good, the true, and the beautiful offers protection against premature certainty and rigidity and provides a source of correctives. Humanism simultaneously and indistinguishably cherishes the *unity* of purpose associated with life's highest potential and the *diversity* that must of necessity characterize particular attempts to realize it. At their best, moral and cultural creativity affirm the unity by ordering and dignifying the diversity and affirm the diversity by varying and enriching the unity. The union of universality and particularity does not belong only to some special sphere beyond ordinary human existence. It is a potentiality of everyday life. It *is* ordinary life making the best of available circumstances. Even in the most adverse situations, the particular and the universal can come together.

In the First World War trench warfare gave examples of unspeakable horror and suffering. This was a hell of human making. But even then a reconciliation of unity and diversity was possible. The higher potentiality of life could make use even of these abominable circumstances. On Christmas Eve the shelling and the fighting stopped along parts of the front. A quiet descended over the barbed, muddy, bloody battlefield. In the quiet, English soldiers could hear their German counterparts singing "Stille Nacht." And the English responded by singing "Silent Night." In some places enemies got out of their trenches and met in no-man's-land.

CHAPTER FOUR

The Living Past

The preceding chapters have presented a thesis regarding the possibility of peaceful relations among cultures and peoples: that a more than temporary and superficial rapprochement will require sustained efforts by different societies to moderate whatever undermines mutual respect and tolerance within each and to marshal their own best moral and cultural resources so that the highest common ground may be cultivated. A cosmopolitan willingness to explore what is impressive, or just simply charming, about other cultures serves peace, but it also holds out the promise of an expanded and deepened human existence. In the shrinking world of today, economic and political advantage alone demands this kind of effort.

To develop this thesis further more attention must be paid to the meaning and origin of cultural identities and to how they relate to the highest common ground. By means of this inquiry we shall continue to pursue the underlying philosophical issue of particularity and universality.

There can be no question of societies giving up their distinctiveness. The history of a people profoundly affects its demeanor and its potential, shaping it in countless ways, most of which are invisible to the superficial glance. A people's past is a source of social cohesion, strength, and creativity, a heritage whose greatest achievements need to be understood anew by each generation and made relevant to new circumstances. The Italian philosopher Benedetto Croce (1866–1952), one of the truly great minds of the twentieth century, writes:

> Historical culture has for its object the keeping alive of the consciousness which human society has of its own past, that is, of

its present, that is, of itself, and to furnish it with what is always required in the choice of the paths it is to follow, namely to keep in readiness for it whatever may be useful for it in this respect in the future.[1]

History is what brought a people to the present point. To understand the past is to understand oneself and contemporary society better. To study history does not serve an antiquarian purpose but is the necessary foundation for well-informed, wise action. As Croce says, "Historical science and culture in all its detailed elaboration exists for the purpose of maintaining and developing the active and civilized life of human society."[2]

Each people has less than admirable traits and inheritances of which it would do well to try to divest itself, but a people also cannot give its best without being itself, without its present efforts somehow expressing, or being adapted to, its historically evolved cultural identity. Every other kind of effort would be mechanical imitation of alien patterns, an artificial appendage possibly destructive of that identity.

All great human accomplishments bear a national or personal imprint, but in their humane significance they also transcend particularity. In these accomplishments of action, thought, and imagination, what is historically distinct, concrete, and particular becomes the vehicle for goodness, truth, or beauty, thus strengthening the sense of universality. The latter is not some kind of abstraction achieved by emptying experience of particularity. For all of their heavy dependence on history, strong cultures are not static, frozen in a particular

1. Benedetto Croce, *History as the Story of Liberty* (Rome: Laterza, 1938; trans. Sylvia Sprigge, rev. Folke Leander and Claes G. Ryn, Indianapolis: Liberty Fund, 2000), 218. Croce inherited wealth and so could work throughout his life as an independent scholar. For forty years he edited his own journal, *La critica*. In the huge corpus of his writing, three highly important early books can be said to contain his central philosophical ideas: *Aesthetic* (1902), *Logic* (1908), and *The Philosophy of the Practical* (1908). Croce became famous for his early aesthetics, which could be cited in support of the notion of art for art's sake, but he also revised and expanded his thinking in this area in ways that made it compatible with Irving Babbitt's idea of the moral imagination as the mark of great art. Though most widely known for his aesthetics, Croce's work in the theory of knowledge and in ethics are at least as deserving of attention.

2. Ibid., 7.

mold. To be a life-giving force, historically formed identities must develop to meet the needs of time and place. Cultural continuity itself requires change. As Edmund Burke says with regard to the political order, "A state without the means of some change is without the means of its conservation." In the same vein, Burke writes admiringly about the adaptability of the constitutional system that had emerged in England: "In what we improve we are never wholly new; in what we retain we are never wholly obsolete." Faithfulness to a cultural heritage involves rejuvenation and revision. In the words of Croce, "Everything lasts only in so far as everything changes." Irving Babbitt describes our general sense of reality as "a oneness that is always changing."[3]

The great civilizations have brought forth works of art, thought, and conduct that attract the deep admiration of later generations. It is in a sense desirable and essential to try to imitate these models of the past, but imitation in the proper humanist sense is not, as Croce points out, "a mere copying or repetition." Such imitation is also "variation, competition and renovation." It is imitation not of "the thing" but of its method and informing value. Babbitt admires Burke because the latter saw "how much of the wisdom of life consists in an imaginative assumption of the experience of the past in such fashion as to bring it to bear as a living force upon the present."[4]

The imagination plays a crucial role by letting new generations and individuals accommodate the models and insights of their heritage within their own experiences, which is a process of adaptation and creativity. In this way, they make the best of the past genuinely their own and thereby make it an inspiring force in the here and now. The absorption of the heritage enriches the present, ultimately because it helps capture universality. In so doing it does in a sense create independence from the past. Though deeply indebted to the exemplars of a tradition, a creative individual, Croce writes, "works afresh from

3. Edmund Burke, *Reflections on the Revolution in France* (Indianapolis: Hackett Publishing Company, 1987), 19, 30; Croce, *Story of Liberty,* 302; Babbitt, *Rousseau and Romanticism,* lxxiii (emphasis in original).

4. Croce, *Story of Liberty,* 355; Irving Babbitt, *Democracy and Leadership* (New York: Houghton Mifflin, 1924; with a new foreword, Indianapolis: Liberty Classics, 1979), 127–28.

his own wits and does not cling to a model, or (which is the same thing) does not cling strictly speaking to the model, but to law which it exemplifies, and therefore he attains to the eternal founts of the Spirit."[5]

Another way of expressing this idea is that unity and diversity imply and require each other. The unity and continuity of the historical heritage will harden and eventually become brittle if it is not embodied in ever-new creative efforts to apply the past. Diverse individual efforts that are not unified by the higher purpose conveyed by the historical heritage will produce mere idiosyncrasy and anarchy.

To argue, as is being done here, that the present depends upon and develops the past and that universality manifests itself historically is not the same as to assert that a sense of the universal emerges from historical continuity of any kind whatever. History abounds with warped, provincial, or idiosyncratic views and practices that have nevertheless acquired some continuity and survived for a rather long time. The quest for the universal is a never-ending process of discriminating among the products of history that is guided by fresh intuition of universal values. This process involves constant selection among the models of the past to see which can help inspire, articulate, and enrich the intuition. This important subject will be taken up again after some related issues have been explored.

No harmony among cultures would result from their trying to erase their distinctive elements and adopt a single model. A people that loses its past loses its sense of identity, self-respect, and direction as well as its creativity. Neither would harmony among peoples result from some easy blending of diverse traits or from a sentimental "brotherhood of man." Superficial attempts to surpass and replace traditional structures only create new opportunities for the darker side of human nature to assert itself. For example, abandoning traditional restraints on human conduct and trusting in the goodness of man may unleash egotism and cruelty. Nor would harmony be brought about by external manipulation, although, needless to say, social, political, and economic measures, national and international, can assist the task. The greatest

5. Croce, *Story of Liberty*, 355.

need for the longer run is that the best resources of particular peoples, as identified by their most cultivated and perceptive representatives, be marshaled so that in the shaping of character, mind, and imagination the spirit of universality will become more discernible and so that individuals and cultures will be able to meet on the highest common ground. How "the best" is known and realized will be discussed at greater length later.[6]

The highest common ground is a life-giving, dynamic center of values. It does not obliterate cultural identities but harmonizes them, letting the diversity enrich the unity. Humanism is a convenient term for the moral and cultural discipline and sensibility through which unity and diversity are reconciled and contribute to a flowering of civilization. In its recognition that different ways are possible toward the center, humanism incorporates, restrains, and deepens multiculturalism.

Those who would like to foster a spirit of humanism today must face a special complication within and among cultures in the modern world—a tension between traditional ways of living and thinking associated with a religious and moral heritage and antitraditional ways of living and thinking associated with modern scientific and technological civilization. In the Western world especially, it has long been widely assumed that a culture of enlightenment of the sort that took hold in the eighteenth century will eventually reconstitute all societies on an allegedly rational basis. According to this view, older moral and religious beliefs are forms of superstition and should be abandoned together with related social patterns. Westerners and non-Westerners alike should free themselves of a premodern heritage that stands in the way of progress.

6. The subject has been addressed in considerable depth in previous works by this author. See, in particular, Ryn, *Will, Imagination and Reason,* which explores the moral, aesthetical, and logical dimensions of universality. For a discussion of the moral core of universality, specifically, the notion of ethical will, see esp. chs. 1, 8, and 9. Moral universality is related to social and political problems in Claes G. Ryn, *Democracy and the Ethical Life,* 2d enl. ed (Baton Rouge: Louisiana State University Press, 1978; Washington, D.C.: Catholic University of America Press, 1990). See esp. chs. 1, 3, and 4. For an exploration of ethical universality as historically evolving, see ch. 13.

One does not have to reject all aspects of the Enlightenment mind to find its understanding of the origins and prospects of social and international order unsatisfactory. It does not confront the human moral predicament with sufficient realism and historical understanding. Its ideas about man and society are too abstractly intellectual and caught up in the present. Enlightenment intellectuals are usually prone to wishful thinking and to vagueness about the sources for various attitudes that they deem desirable, such as respect and tolerance for other human beings. To a considerable extent, they hold to behavioral preferences inherited from the older moral and religious systems but while rejecting the way in which those systems understood the origins of good conduct. The preferred attitudes are believed to emanate somehow from intellectual enlightenment itself, an assumption that exemplifies a lack of historical understanding. As discussed earlier, modern rationalists sometimes combine a faith in science and rational investigations with a Rousseauistic belief in man's natural goodness. They assume that desirable human traits do not have to be deliberately fostered but will develop naturally provided that human society is properly constructed so that human beings can live out their predisposition to goodness. The Enlightenment mind greatly underestimates the depth of the moral and cultural problems of civilized life, specifically, the difficulty of achieving self-restraint and order.

Though they are in some ways parasitic on an older moral and religious heritage, Enlightenment progressives do not accept what that heritage assumes about man's moral condition. According to that older view, what is necessary for the individual and society to become more harmonious and civilized is for individuals to resist the self-indulgence that puts them at odds with other human beings and to make the best of their own gifts. Healthy family life and other civilizing forces such as education can assist the effort to achieve personal excellence—are indeed indispensable—but only sustained effort by individuals can improve the common life. According to the traditional understanding, the moral struggle with self, the slow development of character, is only a part of the protracted work of humanizing existence, but it is the part on which all the others—intellectual, aesthetical, political,

and economic—ultimately depend for their health. Sociopolitical arrangements can aid but not replace inner moral striving.

That this ancient view should not be as popular as modern rationalistic or romantic notions of progress and peace is not difficult
to understand, for it places the burden of responsibility squarely on
the shoulders of the individual. It makes reform of self the precondition for improving social life. Rationalism and Rousseauism are more
comfortable to the particular person in that they emphasize abstract
ratiocination or allegedly beautiful sentiment and corresponding political reform as the way to improving human existence, none of which
requires painful moral self-scrutiny or prolonged difficult personal action upon self. Human beings tend to shrink from the expenditure of
energy necessary for building and maintaining civilized life, and they
are masters at inventing excuses for avoiding strenuous effort, indeed
often spend more time at that task than on the needed work.

One of the great dangers of the modern technocratic-commercial
society, at least in its present Western form, is that it neglects the
formation of character and tends to produce narrowly educated human beings with superficial interests and tastes. Giving precedence to
science and mathematics and to other subjects only in so far as they
may be economically useful or helpful in securing transitory pleasures,
Western society has drifted far from the old Greek notion of *schole,*
the classical discipline that aimed to form and refine the whole person
and to prepare the person for the higher life of the good, the true, and
the beautiful. To pursue education and self-education, most especially
in the moral life, in order to achieve a more deeply satisfying existence
has come to seem intolerably onerous as well as archaic.

The reasons for the reluctance to undertake such discipline, besides
the laziness endemic to the human race, are manifold. They include
unwillingness to accept traditional religious and moral dogma and a
resulting abandonment not just of doctrinal formulations but of the
substance of the kind of life to which dogma referred. It has proven
difficult for Western man to hold on to spiritual and moral truth while
rejecting the doctrinal rigidity with which that truth has sometimes
become associated. This inability to adapt and reformulate exemplifies

a major weakness in Western civilization, a tendency to overintellectualize issues of religion and morality and to neglect the centrality
of action. Some strains of Christianity, such as the belief that man is
utterly dependent on divine grace for his own salvation, which gained
new strength in the Protestant Reformation, became in time for many
an excuse not to place any sustained and heavy emphasis on the need
for personal moral effort, however much Protestant theologians and
moral philosophers would reject such a passive attitude. Romanticism
from the eighteenth century to the present has contributed even more
powerfully to the same kind of reluctance to undertake self-reform by
making sentimental imagination rather than will-action the defining
attribute of real morality. Trust in science has been yet another way of
diverting attention from the need for personal self-discipline.

Today's Western society gives short shrift to the kind of upbringing
and education that might sensitize people to the common human
ground. Though it often raises what it considers moral questions, it
does so not in terms of individual character but in collectivistic and
sentimental terms that imply a need for government-sponsored social
reconstruction. For the rest, today's society lets science and utilitarian and commercial purposes provide a common language and frame
of reference. It treats moral and cultural questions of the more traditional type as belonging to the private and subjective sphere, indicating
thereby that such questions have no universal significance and can be
safely left to personal whim. As people lose the sense that life has
a deeper, enduring purpose, they are increasingly inclined to seek
enjoyment in passing pleasures and to demand instant gratification.
While deriving a semblance of order from externally induced collective morality and the routines and structures of the technocratic-
commercial society, to some extent also from lingering traditional
patterns of life, they are prone, especially in their private lives, to
following the strongest impulse of the moment. Fashion, especially
as shaped by the entertainment industry, and advertising powerfully
affect their tastes.

The personal lives of many modern human beings brings to mind
the kind of personality that Plato associates with "democratic" society.

The Republic may be criticized for a one-sided view of popular government, but its account of "democratic man" appears to describe strong trends in today's Western society:

> [Democratic man] lives from day to day, indulging the pleasure of the moment. One day it's wine, women and song, the next water to drink and a strict diet; one day it's hard physical training, the next indolence and careless ease, and then a period of philosophic study. Often he takes to politics and keeps jumping to his feet and saying or doing whatever comes into his head. Sometimes all his ambitions and efforts are military, sometimes they are all directed at success in business. There's no order or restraint in his life, and he reckons his way of living is pleasant, free and happy.[7]

To most Western "liberal" pluralists and to postmodernists and multiculturalists this kind of proliferation of variety and rejection of traditional moral and cultural order seems a triumph for liberty and diversity. To Plato, in contrast, the flimsiness and unsteadiness of "democratic man" indicate that this type of person is morally in a highly precarious condition and is very far from understanding the higher values of life. Though this man appears at first to be not precisely a sinister character, his lack of inner restraint finally unleashes the very worst human potentialities. His self-absorption becomes ruthless and tyrannical.

If Plato's analysis has any validity, and if individuals of this kind are in fact common in modern societies, this represents a major problem for peace both within and among societies. People unaccustomed to heeding a common human standard will behave with tolerance and consideration for others only if they believe that doing so will advance their own pleasure-seeking or if they are forced to do so by external pressure. This is but one of the reasons why proponents of humanism and international peace must try to reawaken a sense of moral realism in their societies and work to strengthen the awareness of the real preconditions for responsible conduct.

---

7. Plato, *The Republic,* 2d rev. ed. (New York: Penguin Books, 1987), 381 (561c–e).

Both in the East and the West some regard modern technological civilization and the form of production it has made possible as incompatible with a humane society, but it is romantically fanciful to dream of abandoning the scientific and economic advances of the last two centuries. The proper task, it would appear, is to work to spread a spirit of humanism throughout society and to humanize science and economic activity, making them means to the higher ends of civilization. This work is not, as should be clear from previous arguments, a matter of merely reviving and disseminating traditional beliefs. Those beliefs need critical and discriminating scrutiny, and must, to the extent that they remain valid, be restated in ways that can be understood and accepted in the contemporary world.

People who simply assume that present society is the culmination of human development imagine that repairing to history could only retard further advancement, but the past is an indispensable source of insight regarding the ultimate values of human existence. Recovering such insight becomes a stimulus for action in the present. Croce writes, "It is an illusion to fear that consciousness of the past discourages the will to new things, when the truth is that the more energetically the past is known, the more energetic is the impetus to go beyond it and so progress."[8] Today old insight needs to be developed and extended so as both to revise Enlightenment thinking and to incorporate what is valid in it. Without a systematic effort to humanize modern civilization mankind will not only fail to reach the highest ground but will move toward an ever more volatile and dangerous international situation.

8. Croce, *Story of Liberty,* 217–18.

CHAPTER FIVE

A Common Ethical Center

Peace among cultures may be possible in the twenty-first century only if their various elites cultivate the discipline and sensibility of cosmopolitan humanism and are able to impart to their respective peoples some awareness of the shared higher ground of mankind. Each society needs leadership that inspires its people to live up to its own highest moral and cultural standards and that draws attention to how those standards correspond to the aspirations of other peoples. Elites—all those individuals and groups in a variety of social roles who command the special respect and admiration of others and who can therefore affect the general direction of life—must find existential, as distinguished from merely transitory and convenient, reasons for having good relations with other peoples. For more than superficial affinities to develop among representatives of different societies there must be a substantial element of agreement regarding basic issues of life.

In the twentieth century, "equality" became the preeminent professed social and political value of Western man. The existence of elites with influence greater than that of the common man was widely condemned, at least in theory. Egalitarian ideology became, in the twentieth century especially, the justification for major social change, but aspects of that change merely confirmed what egalitarianism denies in theory, that no society or organization can function without leadership. People of special gifts and particular willpower inevitably acquire more influence than others. The age of equality has not meant the triumph of equality in practice. Old elites have been removed or demoted, but others have immediately taken their places. New class structures, including ones of considerable rigidity, have been created that belie the possibility of a society without elites. In fact, egalitarianism can be said to have in some respects *increased* the power of elites over the common people. This is the case partly because egalitarian social reconstruction has helped destroy the decentralized society with its dispersed elites and made it less and less possible to present grievances against a ruling elite to competing elites. In the societies officially most strongly dedicated to egalitarian ideology, the old Soviet Union, for example, *in*equalities were especially glaring. The Soviet *nomenklatura* (the sociopolitical stratum given special economic and other benefits), to say nothing of the very highest political elites, formed a highly privileged class separate from the common people, and it was not possible for others to appeal their misrule or brutality.

Elites are often blatantly self-serving, arbitrary, or ruthless, but the notion of doing away with them is a figment of the naive, romantic imagination. What is possible is for elites of various kinds—political, economic, intellectual, artistic, religious, scientific, etc.—to be more or less humane and dispersed. For elites to embody the very highest standards of their respective societies and to exist at different levels and in numerous shapes adjusted to a broad range of human activities and concerns is essential to the well-being of those societies. Such diversified leadership and the resulting pressure to live up to high expectations is the natural breeding ground for the kind of cosmopolitan humanism that is advocated here. What is exemplary in one culture tends to be synergic with what is exemplary in another.[1]

Though cultures are bound to differ in how they approach and express goodness, truth, and beauty, there is among them, as previously discussed, also a historical confluence of moral and cultural sensibility of great potential significance for the future. The ancient civilizations of the world have been in far-reaching agreement about what constitutes admirable human traits. Of particular relevance in a discussion of prospects for peace is the widely shared belief that self-restraint and humility are defining attributes of the admirable person. This theme was long pervasive in the West. The ancient Greeks warned against

1. For a discussion of the inevitability of political elites, with emphasis on the ethical dimension of the subject, see Ryn, *Democracy and Ethical Life,* esp. parts 3 and 4.

the arrogance of *hubris,* against believing oneself the equal of the gods. Remember that you are a mere human! In Sophocles's drama *King Oedipus,* a highly intelligent and otherwise admirable but also rash and arrogant ruler is brought down by *nemesis.* He pierces his own eyes in recognition of and punishment for his human blindness. The danger of pride has been stressed even more in Christianity, which has also emphasized that our primary moral obligation is not pointing out weaknesses in others and asking them to change, but diligently attending to our own weaknesses. Christianity roundly condemns the conceit and moral evasiveness of finding fault in others. In the words of Jesus of Nazareth,

> Do not judge others, so that God will not judge you. . . . Why, then, do you look at the speck in your brother's eye, and pay no attention to the log in your own eye? How dare you say to your brother, "Please, let me take that speck out of your eye," when you have a log in your own eye? You hypocrite! Take the log out of your own eye first, and then you will be able to see and take the speck out of your brother's eye.[2]

If the elites of different cultures are able to control their own arrogant presumptions of superiority and to recognize commonalities in respect to what ultimately makes life worth living, they may not only come to respect other societies but wish to be morally and culturally enriched by them. It should be obvious from the argument presented here that such rapprochement could not be accomplished through the type of "international understanding" that combines sentimental gestures with the flimsy knowledge of tourists. Besides a predisposition to self-control and humility, real understanding among cultures presupposes sustained study and other familiarity. A person does not have to be an orthodox religious or moral traditionalist or oppose all elements of Enlightenment civilization to recognize that a genuine ecumenism is not based on assent to abstract intellectual propositions or adoption of romantic notions about people being naturally prone to loving one another. Neither does one have to dismiss the importance

2. Matt. 6:1–5.

of political and economic agreements for national and international well-being in order to assert that there is no substitute for the elites of various societies setting high moral and cultural examples for their own people.

Though the point has in a way already been made, it may be useful to emphasize that the highest common ground between societies and civilizations must not be confused with whatever consensus may exist among peoples or societies at a particular time. The "mainstream" of opinion is sometimes in sharp conflict with humanity's highest standards. This kind of consensus may be little more than superficial fashionable views or a "herd" mentality whipped up by demagogues. Neither should the humility just described be confused with a pursuit of mediocrity or with the kind of "slave morality" that Nietzsche condemned. Genuine humility is fully compatible with challenging not only mediocrity but the prevalent moral, aesthetical, and intellectual standards of highbrow culture. Those who wish to refresh and renew society's sense of goodness, truth, or beauty must to some extent defy and surpass conventional beliefs. Genuine humility does not suppress creativity. It does the opposite by checking the human propensity for conceited self-absorption and for underestimating the debt that new creativity owes to the past.

In trying to elucidate the ethical dimension of the common human ground it is appropriate to adopt an ecumenical approach and explore what the great moral and religious systems of mankind have in common. Possible then is a cross-cultural discussion that is centered not on issues of doctrinal divergence but on the concrete, *experiential* content of the moral and religious life of different societies. Broad areas of agreement are discernible. To be meaningful, an ecumenical exchange of views does not have to be preceded by agreement on disputed theological and other dogmas. To place theological doctrine, including conceptions said to be based on revelation, at the center of attention is to induce defensiveness or presumptions of superiority on the various sides of the debate and to discourage discussion before it has had a chance to begin. That theologians and others have placed special interpretations upon the experiential evidence of the moral and religious life need not stand in the way of going deeply into that evidence in a philosophical manner. It is possible to arrive at far-reaching conclusions without taking a stand on the contested dogmas. Besides having obvious practical advantages, this ecumenical approach is congenial to the philosophical mind, which wants to rest judgments on evidence available to humanity in general.

The great moral and religious systems coincide in that they give primacy to a power that transcends the desires of individual human beings and orders life to a higher purpose. This power has been interpreted in special ways by representatives of different faiths, but the resulting doctrines of ethics and theology give definite theoretical form to something that is known first of all in experience. The presence in man of a special will that wills the universal, what is good for its own sake, is a matter of direct, immediate personal awareness, and this will can be studied in its actual influence on human behavior without assuming the validity of any particular doctrines. Some individuals have an especially strong awareness of this higher power, but though it manifests itself in unique ways in different persons due to their special circumstances, its authority is felt to transcend individuality. The human race as a whole has testified to its existence over the centuries. Behind the varied specifics of particular moral systems and behind the liturgical and doctrinal peculiarities of particular religions the serious and open-minded observer is able to discern a single centering power that calls human beings to a life of righteousness or, in a few cases, even to holiness. There exists at the very core of human experience a special quality of will, a fundamental source of goodness and happiness, which human beings can make progressively their own. This higher will has been widely identified with God, in Christianity with a personal deity, but in some parts of the world and sometimes also in the West it has been regarded not as an attribute of a separate divine personality but as what is highest in man: a higher self that is at once intensely personal and common to all men, common though often unheeded. This self stands in constant opposition to whatever demeans human existence; it is the potentiality for goodness and union within and among human beings. Because different cultures have spoken of this higher self in many different ways, referring to it in nonsectarian language is appropriate to ecumenical discussion. Babbitt often calls it the "inner check" to indicate that in a crucial respect it is a restraint upon impulse. His choice of that term also suggests his high respect for Eastern moral and religious insight.[3]

One reason for Babbitt's interest in Buddhism is that it seems to him a corrective to a tendency in Western Christianity to become overly dogmatic and metaphysical. Buddhism places less stress on ratiocination than it does on the need to act to change self. Being right on doctrine is for Buddhism less important than acting rightly. Babbitt writes, "If the Far East has been comparatively free from casuistry, obscurantism, and intolerance, the credit is due in no small measure to Buddha." Babbitt reprimands Westerners who simply assume their superiority over Easterners in moral and religious matters. Though critical of some aspects of Confucianism, such as excessive formalism, Babbitt thinks Confucianism shares a salutary feature with Buddhism: "The comparative absence of dogma in the humanism of Confucius and the religion of Buddha can scarcely be regarded as an inferiority." Like many other commentators on morality and religion, such as Eric Voegelin, Babbitt sometimes goes too far in minimizing the role of intellect and philosophy in that part of life, or gives the *appearance* of doing so, but moral and religious philosophy badly need the kind of close attention to experiential evidence, including the role of practical willing, that he urges.[4]

---

3. The common element in the higher religions is discussed in Irving Babbitt, "Buddha and the Occident," in *The Dhammapada*. Babbitt assumes that genuinely religious striving can assume different forms in different cultural contexts, but his view of its central general characteristics is considerably more restrictive and discriminating than that of William James, for example, whose notion of religion is drawn from a "pluralism" of experience that looks too much like a mishmash. In his study of religion James treats sober and balanced religious experience together with emotional disturbance and extravagance of various kinds without providing an adequate criterion for telling them apart. See William James, *The Varieties of Religious Experience* (New York: Collier Books, 1961).

The "inner check" is discussed in all of Babbitt's books, including *Rousseau and Romanticism* and *Democracy and Leadership*. For a thorough philosophical explication and critique of this idea, see Ryn, *Will, Imagination and Reason.*

4. Babbitt, "Buddha and the Occident," 70, 68. For a critique of Babbitt's flawed understanding of reason and for an in-depth explication of the philosophical rationality that Babbitt (like most other thinkers of the twentieth century) neglects, see Ryn, *Will, Imagination and Reason,* esp. chs. 4–7.

Whatever the disagreements between East and West in these matters, the traditional cultures regard the higher will in much the same way. Though this will is respected more by some individuals than by others and is wholly denied by some, it draws humanity toward a common moral center. This unification can assume two different, though closely related, forms, leading individuals to adopt one of two primary orientations. The one may be called humanistic because it aims at a more humane worldly existence, one in which the good, the true, and the beautiful are more richly represented. Some may consider this orientation religious in a broad sense because it regards its ultimate inspiration as universal. The other manifestation of the higher will is religious in the strictest possible meaning of that word; it is an attempt to "overcome" the ordinary world. All exercise of the higher will is an effort to drive from the world human desires that threaten a more truly civilized, more deeply rewarding existence, but some few individuals feel called to attempt an even more complete and strenuous moral-spiritual discipline. They try to go beyond checking desires incompatible with humane civilization. This more intense and demanding striving may be defined in terms of otherworldliness or holiness. It is exemplified by monks and nuns. This is the rare and special kind of life to whose final purpose both the East and the West have referred in phrases like "renouncing the world" or "dying to the world." In the East the very culmination of the attempted severing of the ties to ordinary human existence has been called "Nirvana." A Christian phrase for what lies at the end of the otherworldly striving and that expresses also the Eastern view is "a peace that passeth understanding." On this elevated religious plane fractious and clamoring human desires are overcome, and conflict is no more.

It should be stated explicitly that a philosophical observer may approach this part of human experience with great interest and understanding and even recognize the intrinsic authority of the higher will without also endorsing the special claims of a particular faith. Accepting the evidence of a higher will might be regarded by some as by itself indicative of a religious outlook, but it needs to be understood that "religion" is a word of many meanings and that a person acknowledging the existence of moral universality may still be unable to accept many of the specific beliefs of traditional sects or churches. Addressing these subjects the philosopher does not restrict his audience to believers. He feels the need to present concrete evidence that can be taken seriously not only by believers but also by skeptics who are open-minded though not prepared to accept moral and religious claims on authority.

Modern Western positivism is inadequate to the study of moral and religious questions and related questions of human relevance. Positivism refuses to consider evidence that is not amenable to treatment by the methods of the natural sciences or some imitation of them in the humanities and social sciences. A genuine philosopher, as distinguished from a dogmatist, is willing to accept the challenge that moral and religious beliefs be subjected to scrutiny by the skeptical intellect. The demand for proof does not, as positivists assume, by itself refute the old insights. These find considerable support in man's self-experience now and throughout history. That body of evidence is available for inspection by the philosophical intellect.

Babbitt proposes that the proper methodology for the study of human nature be labeled "a more complete positivism." This ill-chosen and confusing term does not even convey what he has in mind, which is that scholars should consider evidence that has been arbitrarily excluded by positivistic methodology. Babbitt's mistake is to think that this objective could be served by broadening a generally positivistic methodology. Really to expand and deepen the study of man and to attend carefully to the inner life, which is indeed an urgent need, is not to revise positivism but to abandon it. What is appropriate to the study of man as a moral, religious, artistic, and intellectual being is science of a wholly different, philosophical kind. The needed opening-up to the facts of human self-experience entails *replacing* positivism with a method that takes man's inner life seriously. Faithfully examining the distinctly human sphere involves an "empiricism" or "phenomenology" of its own but has nothing to do with positivism. The human sphere is not accessible by scientistic methods, but it is fully accessible by disciplined, philosophical-historical humanistic inquiry. Many old truths that became bound up with moral or religious doctrine and were rejected by skeptics in that form can be revalidated on the basis of the shared experience of the human race and restated in a form that is acceptable and even persuasive to honest skeptics, those who are truly devoted to the critical intellect and the examination of evidence and who therefore abjure dogmatic rationalism. To explore the body of evidence pertaining to a moral-spiritual center of human existence is itself a source of unity.[5]

The literary and other cultural treasures of mankind are also indispensable to human self-understanding. The imaginative masterminds have seen more deeply than others into the human condition. This is the case even though art sometimes draws people into visions of life that are warped and degrading but that nevertheless become influential because of their imaginative power. Truly great art is different. What Babbitt, borrowing a term from Edmund Burke, calls "the moral imagination" shows us something of life as it really is, both in its higher and lower manifestations. It conveys a sense of the order and purpose of existence. Though wholly nondidactic, such art lifts the human spirit and strengthens man for the higher life. It should be added that the more prosaic and scholarly students of humanity also depend in the end, for good or ill, on the imaginative masterminds for their sense of direction and proportion. Art and scholarship are wholly different modes of approaching life, but for the scholar to see his facts more than superficially and in their larger context and to be able therefore to say something important, he, like the rest of us, needs an imagination sensitized and deepened by the great artists.

Humanity manifests endless variety; all individuals and societies have distinctive traits. The main point of this chapter is that this diversity coexists with, blends with, and is guided by a universal human element, which, though it has additional dimensions, is constituted most fundamentally by a special kind of will. This centering power need not be approached in dogmatic, confessional terms. It is an experiential

5. A philosophical-historical methodology for the study of man is set forth systematically and at length in Ryn, *Will, Imagination and Reason,* which is an attempt to reconstitute the epistemology of the humanities and social sciences.

reality accessible to scrutiny by the philosophical mind, which is an ecumenical mind. The same reality is known intuitively by the highest form of the artistic imagination. The latter helps orient the mind to the potentiality that promises the most deeply rewarding and satisfying existence.

CHAPTER SIX

Dubious Conceptions of Unity

To reduce the danger of clashes between civilizations the Harvard political scientist Samuel Huntington has recommended that "all civilizations should search for and attempt to expand the values, institutions, and practices they have in common with peoples of other civilizations."[1] This view might at first blush seem not dissimilar to the one presented here, but it is seriously deficient in at least one important respect. Huntington avoids the urgent need to discriminate between commonalities that are conducive to peaceful relations, in the short or the long run, and those that are not. Far from always improving relations, having preferences or practices in common may lead in just the opposite direction. For societies to have in common a single-minded pursuit of economic advantage, for example, is likely to produce conflict. More generally, peace is not served by having in common such tendencies as lack of moderation and prudence, unreasonable expectations, lack of critical perspective, narrowness of mind, and nationalistic partisanship. One could easily draw up a lengthy list of present "commonalities" that undermine rather than strengthen the basis for harmonious relations. Many in the West celebrate the improved communications in today's world. They are less interested in the quality of what is being communicated. Sometimes the communication across cultures is even detrimental to improved relations. Take as but one example television news stories about world events that are produced and reported by individuals of superficial views and broadcast around the world in segments of a few minutes' duration.

1. Samuel Huntington, *The Clash of Civilizations and the Remaking of World Order* (New York: Simon & Schuster, 1996), 320.

The world according to CNN may indeed create commonalities in how the world is viewed, but the spread of shallow and highly biased perceptions does not advance peace. One troublesome aspect of the prominence of "news" in international relations is that it caters increasingly to the lowest common denominator of popular tastes and is becoming virtually indistinguishable from entertainment. In politics another spreading "commonality" is modern advertising techniques to build support for politicians and governments. Peoples used to accepting simplistic images and appeals may also be vulnerable to campaigns of nationalistic hysteria.

Among the commonalities emerging today, there are a number of troubling cultural trends with long-term implications. In popular culture and entertainment—movies, television programs, music, and so on—the dominant types of imagination tolerate or even glorify human traits exceedingly difficult to reconcile with self-restraint, prudence, refinement, and breadth of vision. These trends create similarities among societies, but they also run counter to good relations and specifically to the need for meeting on the highest moral and cultural ground. Commonalities of this kind threaten to pit the self-indulgence of one people against that of another, which leads to conflict, not peace.

Huntington exhibits a reluctance typical of modern Western liberals to distinguish between what is morally and culturally admirable and what is repugnant, a reluctance that is philosophically disingenuous and inconsistent in that he does assume Western enlightenment to be superior to the lack of it. Acting the role of the enlightened liberal who rejects universalist moral claims, Huntington writes, "In a multicivilizational world the constructive course is to renounce universalism, accept diversity, and seek commonalities." To a policymaker who has to deal with the world as it is, this prescription may look practical, but it neglects precisely what peaceful relations may require most: a willingness and an ability, especially among the world's elites, to recognize a good deal more than "commonalities," namely an existential moral and cultural bond, a common ethical center. That an abstract or sentimental universalism will not meet that need has been argued here at some length. One of the reasons why Huntington wishes to renounce "universalism" is that he has a highly questionable notion of what it might be. Lacking the necessary philosophical understanding, he wrongly assumes that accepting universalism is the same as believing that all peoples should conform to a particular model of life, an assumption that he recognizes as detrimental to international harmony. Universalism, he assumes, "legitimates imperialism."[2] It is to Huntington's credit that he should resist ideas that imply a desire to make the world over in a single image, but he is mistaken in thinking that universalism must be understood in that manner and that it is the enemy of diversity and a multicultural world.

In the higher life of humanity, universality and particularity are in an important sense not irreconcilable; they are compatible and even dependent upon each other. To explicate and defend this thesis remains the central purpose of this book.

It has been suggested here that life contains intrinsically valuable potentialities that can be realized through effort. The notion of universality associated with this view contains no implication that all individuals and societies ought to conform to a single model of life or that universality can be imposed from without through political engineering. To explain further the conception of universality that is being advanced, it may be helpful to contrast it with a universalist ideology that assumes precisely what this conception rejects. The ideology in question is especially influential in the United States. Its representatives believe that a single political system, democracy, is appropriate for all societies and are prone to advocating intervention in societies that do not conform to their preference.

Oddly, many of these intellectuals have become known in America as "neoconservatives." Among these individuals are writers, journalists, and public figures like William Bennett, the late Allan Bloom, Charles Krauthammer, William Kristol, Michael Novak, and Norman Podhoretz. Many of them have been strongly influenced by the late German-American political theorist Leo Strauss, who is the founder of a large and distinctive school of thought. One reason why it has seemed plausible to some to regard individuals like these as conservatives of a kind is that they speak the language of "universal values" and

2. Ibid., 318.

"virtue" and sometimes claim Plato and the classical Greek heritage and even Judeo-Christianity as sources for their thinking. But the label is rather paradoxical, for these intellectuals are often quite dissimilar to traditional American or European conservatives. Their conception of "universal principles" is ahistorical and antitraditionalistic and different also in other ways from that of older conservatives. In fact, in some respects many neoconservatives resemble the French Jacobins of the eighteenth century, the radicals who spearheaded the French Revolution and wanted to spread "freedom, equality, and brotherhood" to the rest of the world. As the champions of a new, superior society, the French Jacobins considered themselves embodiments of virtue. The Jacobin impulse would in time make itself felt in various permutations all over the world. Adopting a kind of Jacobin universalism, many neoconservatives believe that all peoples need and desire a certain type of society and government, the one that those neoconservatives favor. It tells you a great deal about the evolution of Western thought that when self-conscious conservatism originally arose in the Western world it was precisely in reaction *against* Jacobin universalism and more generally against abstract, ahistorical notions of good. It should be added that not all neoconservatives are neo-Jacobins and that some are such only in diluted form.

The claim of some neoconservatives of neo-Jacobin leanings to have Plato as a philosophical authority might make some limited sense in that, in his epistemology, Plato disparages historical particularity and in that he espouses a single standard of political justice. In other ways the claim is highly questionable. Plato was a severe critic of democracy as he understood it. He roundly condemned not only democratic government but also "democratic man," the personality type, whom he saw as animating it. The new Jacobins, by contrast, prescribe democracy for the entire world, usually in combination with what they call "capitalism." They regard this kind of political-economic system as the culmination of mankind's long search for the best society. Some, like the American Roman Catholic writer Michael Novak, even regard this kind of society as divinely sanctioned, a view that contrasts rather sharply with more traditional Christian thought. The latter agreed with Aristotle that all governments should have a concern for the good of the whole but believed that different forms of rule are suited to different circumstances. For the neo-Jacobins, democracy, with "capitalism" and "human rights" as integral parts, defines the ultimate political system. It is, they argue, the system for which mankind has always been searching and is everywhere appropriate. Intellectuals of this mind-set have announced the "end of history," a phrase popularized by Francis Fukuyama, which means that the question of the best way of life has now been settled once and for all. Ideological strife will eventually peter out as people around the world recognize the superiority of democracy. Benevolent governments, especially the United States as the most powerful, should help spread this form of government around the world.[3]

Though this triumphalist universalism often uses traditional-sounding terms like *virtue* and *universal values,* it is in essential respects alien to the older Western tradition. Specifically, the new Jacobinism is hard to reconcile with the view of life and politics held by the Framers of the U.S. Constitution, men who are widely revered still in America, even as the older American political tradition erodes. Although proximate in time, the ideas behind the U.S. Constitution adopted in 1789 and those behind the French Revolution of the same year are widely divergent. The Constitution's Framers had a view of human nature and society radically different from that of Jean-Jacques Rousseau. Nevertheless, partly to appropriate to themselves some of the authority that continues to attach to the old American Constitution, the new Jacobins typically associate what they consider right for all peoples with the "founding principles" of the United States. They simply ignore those parts of the historical record that do not appeal to them and define the founding principles in an ahistorical manner consonant with their own universalist ideology.

Over fifteen years ago, one of their intellectual leaders, Allan Bloom,

---

3. The idea of history's ending has appeared in various forms in the last several decades among modern Western liberals, who would like to believe that their own thoughts about politics and society are the ultimate insights of all humanity. See, for example, Daniel Bell, *The End of Ideology: On the Exhaustion of Political Ideas in the Fifties* (Glencoe, Ill.: Free Press, 1960), or a more recent representative of the genre, Francis Fukuyama, "The End of History," *National Interest* 16 (summer 1989).

one of the best-known disciples of Leo Strauss, provided a striking example of this attempt to redefine the American identity. In what became a best-selling and very influential book, Bloom asserts, "When we Americans speak seriously about politics, we mean that our principles of freedom and equality and the rights based on them are rational and everywhere applicable." "Our story," he proclaims, "is the majestic and triumphant march of freedom and equality." Exhibiting the bias of those who see modern "liberal" political ideas and arrangements as the conclusion to age-old debates, Bloom writes, "There is no intellectual ground remaining for any regime other than democracy." The United States is for Bloom not a historically evolved nation with deep roots in the English and European past but is an intellectual "project" designed according to an ahistorical standard equally applicable to all peoples. "This is a regime founded by philosophers and their students," he asserts. "America is actually nothing but a great stage" on which a theory has been acted out. "There are almost no accidents."[4]

Bloom exemplifies the neo-Jacobins' lack of interest in or resentment of historically formed cultural particularity and their belief that a certain political doctrine is entitled to hegemony, nay, monopoly. On the basis of such thinking, intellectuals and politicians are assigning to the United States a global political task: promoting democracy and human rights. As "an exceptional nation" committed to universal principles, the United States should, in the words of two political intellectuals, have a "foreign policy of national strength and moral assertiveness abroad." American political leaders frequently speak a similar language. President George H. Bush's secretary of state, James Baker, for example, explicitly committed American foreign policy to "enlightenment ideals of universal applicability." After September 11, 2001, President George W. Bush discarded earlier expressed reservations about American interventionism and in a series of speeches and other statements became a strong advocate of American assertiveness abroad in behalf of a virtuous American empire charged with creating a better world. In his view, "There is a value system that cannot

4. Allan Bloom, *The Closing of the American Mind* (New York: Simon & Schuster, 1987), 153, 97, 330, 97.

be compromised, and that is the values we praise. And if the values are good enough for our people, they ought to be good enough for others."[5]

Neo-Jacobin intellectuals claim reason as the basis for their universalism, but theirs is not a reason marked by humility and openness to alternative points of view. You cannot read their statements about America's special role as beneficent global actor without a palpable sense that in their form of universalism the will to power supercedes and controls thought. Ideology replaces philosophy. Jacobins, whether old or new, want to mobilize politically and even militarily in behalf of what they deem good for the peoples of the world. The appeals by today's American Jacobins to Plato are strained because of Plato's low opinion of democracy and because he does not believe that political good can be imposed from without by crusading politicians. Plato's universalism has its own highly questionable aspects, among which is its ahistoricism, but Plato sees moral-political virtue as a rare and rather delicate force originating in the individual soul. He heavily emphasizes protracted moral and intellectual discipline as the source of virtue. Only to the extent that a highly gifted few are able to achieve right order in their souls can a spirit of justice begin to enter society. Philosophical wisdom is for Plato not a product of Jacobin-type rationality but is indistinguishable from a soundness of moral character built up over many years through a subduing and ordering of the passions. Jacobin reason and virtue, by contrast, are blatantly political. They provide a justification for giving power to persons who claim to want to act for the good of mankind. Reason and virtue of this kind do not mainly manifest a desire to control and improve self but a desire to control and improve others. Jacobin universalism, wherever it occurs, does not have the effect of curbing the will to power but of stimulating it.[6]

5. William Kristol and David Brooks, "What Ails Conservatism," *Wall Street Journal,* September 15, 1997; Secretary of State James Baker, speech to the Aspen Institute in Berlin, Germany, June 18, 1991; remarks by President George W. Bush in interview with Bob Woodward, *Washington Post,* November 19, 2002, in Woodward, *Bush at War* (New York: Simon & Schuster, 2002).

6. Perhaps the most insightful discussion of the way in which humanitarian schemes of "service to mankind" mask a will to power is Babbitt, *Democracy and*

It is important to understand that the neo-Jacobin interpretation of America's "founding principles" is willfully misleading. Unlike the leaders of the French Revolution, America's leaders at the time of the War of Independence and the adoption of the Constitution were not interested in ideological crusading. Americans hoped to set a good example for others, not impose their will on other peoples. A central purpose of the U.S. Constitution is to restrain power, both that of the people and that of their representatives. The Framers used the word *democracy* disparagingly for the most part, meaning by it a system marked by demagoguery, opportunism, rabble-rousing, shortsightedness, and irresponsibility. The national government set up by the Constitution was popular in orientation by the standards of the Western world at the time, but it did not envision a majoritarian mass-democracy based on universal suffrage. It provided for quasi-aristocratic representative institutions—the senate, the Supreme Court, the electoral college, and the presidency—which were intended, in the words of *The Federalist,* to "refine and enlarge the public views."[7] The Framers saw a need for responsible officials to articulate the long-term best interests of the people. The Constitution gave no power to the people as an undifferentiated national mass of individuals. It assumed a subdivided and highly decentralized society. If the term *democracy* is used to describe the form of government prescribed by the original U.S. Constitution, it is essential to distinguish between what the present writer has called constitutional democracy and majoritarian, or plebiscitary, democracy. The former is popular rule under self-imposed constitutional restraints, and it employs representative institutions; the latter is popular rule according to the numerical majority of the moment. These forms of popular rule are not slightly different versions of one type of government. They are radically different and imply radically different views of human nature and society. This

---

Leadership. This work is more generally a highly perceptive examination of the ethical and cultural bases of the civilized society and what threatens them in modern Western society.

7. Alexander Hamilton, John Jay, and James Madison, *The Federalist,* ed. George W. Carey and James McClellan (Dubuque, Iowa: Kendall/Hunt Publishers, 1990), 10:47.

author has suggested elsewhere that plebiscitary democracy is inimical to the civilized society. The constitutional form, on the other hand, has very demanding moral, cultural, and intellectual preconditions and cannot be created by simple decree. Different peoples are more or less capable of the restraints and responsibilities required by this form of government. The neo-Jacobins use the term *democracy* rather loosely, with a majoritarian bias, and do not much concern themselves with the crucially important question of whether in particular societies the historical circumstances are suited to responsible popular government.[8]

From the point of view of Jacobin universalism, the historically conditioned diversity of peoples and groups, marked as it typically is by the habits and prejudices of a predemocratic era, appears an obstacle to humanity's realizing its true destiny.[9] Jacobin universalism envisions moral, cultural, and political homogeneity. What Bloom approves as the "American project" represents just this kind of universalism. Giving a highly dubious account of the ideological origins and aims of the United States of America, he writes about its people: "By recognizing and accepting man's natural rights, men found a fundamental basis of unity and sameness. Class, race, religion, national origin or culture all disappear or become dim when bathed in the light of natural rights, which give men common interests and make them truly brothers." Jacobin universality, let it be carefully noted, is at the expense of diversity. In the United States as Bloom prefers to think of it, people are expected "to give up their 'cultural' individuality and make themselves into that universal, abstract being who participates in natural rights." People who do not do so, he asserts, are "doomed to an existence on the fringe."[10]

8. For an extensive discussion of the contrasting forms of popular government and their social and political implications, with an emphasis on ethical issues, see Ryn, *Democracy and Ethical Life*. This book regards plebiscitary, or majoritarian, democracy as ultimately incompatible with the ethical requirements of the civilized society.

9. For an in-depth analysis of the new Jacobinism, see Claes G. Ryn, *America the Virtuous: The Crisis of Democracy and the Quest for Empire* (New Brunswick: Transaction Publishers, 2003).

10. Bloom, *Closing*, 27, 30–31.

The neo-Jacobin fondness for abstract homogeneity and depreca-
tion of historical particularity runs counter to old American attitudes
and actual American history. The Latin phrase *e pluribus unum,* out
of many one, often has been applied to the American political and
social experience, especially to the Constitution, but in that context
the phrase does not signify an intended obliteration of diversity. Americans at the time of the writing of the Constitution deeply cherished
their local independence and diverse traditions and jealously guarded
them against intrusions from the political center. The federal system set
up by the Constitution granted the central government only limited
and shared sovereignty, leaving power for the most part where it had
previously resided, in state and local institutions and, above all, with
the people themselves in their private capacities. The aim of the new
constitutional arrangement was unity *in* diversity or, as it might be
even better phrased in the philosophical context of this book, unity
through diversity. The union of states would help *harmonize* diversity
and draw strength from diversity, not abolish it.

The Framers of the Constitution did not, except in a very limited
way, try to create a single, all-encompassing or exhaustive national purpose. They saw a close connection between maintaining the freedom
they desired and permitting a wide range of interests to express themselves. They hoped that personal responsibility, buttressed at various
levels by institutional "checks and balances," would make it possible
for *different* groups to accommodate and respect one another. Stand-
ing in the Christian tradition, the Framers assumed the importance
of individual moral effort and tolerance. They expected that diversity,
made responsible in the manner described, would not only continue
in the future but would enrich the whole.

That despite these facts of American history Bloom and others of
neo-Jacobin leanings should view the United States as dedicated from
the beginning to an abstract universalism is indicative of the intensity
of their ideological passion. They are committed to unity understood
as centrally induced ideological uniformity. The neo-Jacobins offer a
modern ideological and politicized version of the old Platonic assumption that universality is incompatible with particularity. According to

Plato, the universal, which is the true norm and meaning of existence, lies beyond the phenomenal, historical world. To ascend to the universal human beings must, as far as is possible, shed their particularity. The universal is eternal and unchanging, whereas history, which is forever changeable, is a meaningless flux to be held at bay. Because there is a fundamental enmity between universality and particularity, it is contrary to the pursuit of good for individuals or peoples to cherish their respective traditions or cultivate their uniqueness. The neo-Jacobin disinterest in or hostility toward historically evolved cultural identities has stark political implications. It becomes for them a moral requirement to help sweep away whatever traditional arrangements and practices block the emergence of a homogeneous universal culture—what the neo-Jacobins usually summarize as "democracy." Plato himself was an antidemocratic and almost apolitical thinker, but the intensely political neo-Jacobins find his ahistorical universalism appealing and adjust it to their own conception of political right.

Sadly, the affirmations of diversity made by postmodern multiculturalism do not provide a sound antidote to neo-Jacobinism. This kind of multiculturalism offers weak support for culturally distinct entities and for peace among them. If it were true, as postmodernists argue, that there is no common human ground, no universal purpose of human existence, humanism, for example, would be a meaningless term. Without a shared center of values with reference to which individuals, groups, and societies can limit and order their diversity, differences are bound to place a heavy strain on domestic and international peace. History shows intolerance and ruthless self-aggrandizement to be endemic. In the absence of strong internal moral and cultural checks among those who set the tone in their societies, typical postmodernist and liberal exhortations to be tolerant are very fragile obstacles to conflict. Without a deep-seated sense of common humanity, why should representatives of one culture or society not be expected to try to dominate another for their own benefit? True, enlightened self-interest and concern for survival can be powerful inducements to self-restraint, as they were during the Cold War, which did not become a nuclear war. A Western liberal might thus put his trust in sophisticated selfishness to produce tolerance and keep the peace.

But a "balance of terror," the threat of mutual annihilation, is not typical of relations among groups and nations. Most of the time the danger is that the strong will be tempted to dominate, mistreat, or destroy the weak. What will check this inclination? Granted, even in a situation in which a potential aggressor does not need to risk annihilation, enlightened self-interest is likely to play a moderating role. There are costs to any conflict. What must not be overlooked is that this kind of prudence depends on an already existing sense of what is and what is not a proper way to treat other human beings. That sense has everything to do with the moral traditions of the particular society and is frequently an aspect of religious belief. Suppose that, in accordance with postmodernism or liberal moral relativism, the notion of an enduring higher purpose of human life is completely discarded and human beings lose or suppress an older sense of moral limits. How, in a world where nothing is thought to be universal and obligatory and there are only competing subjective preferences, could "enlightened" self-interest even be defined? Why should peace or even survival be expected to remain preferred goals? In human history war and death-defying heroics have sometimes held considerable appeal for many. In assuming the continuation of a desire for peace and tolerance, postmodernists and others rely parasitically on an older view of life, one that they are attempting to replace. All things considered, it should come as no surprise if persons who recognize no standard of conduct beyond their own present inclinations should start to belittle other peoples and see other individuals and groups as properly their servants or subjects.

It is troublesome that at this time of growing interaction between cultures the Western world should be so strongly influenced on the one side by an ideological imperialism ostensibly based on "universal values," and on the other side by a radical moral relativism or nihilism. The choice between them is a false one. In at least one respect the two orientations have more in common than might first appear. They are both manifestations of a disinclination to place limits on one's own desires. The new Jacobins can be accused of dressing up in humanitarian garb a desire to dominate other people. The postmodernist rejection of all higher norms also may be seen as removing obstacles to enacting one's own subjective wishes. Because human beings are so strongly biased in their own favor, it makes little difference in practice whether partisan personal desires are assumed to be sanctioned by universal values, as with the neo-Jacobins, or to be simply permitted by the absence of higher norms, as with the postmodern multiculturalists. It is relevant in this context that many of the Straussians who advocate universal right and democracy regard this advocacy as intended for public consumption only; in private they are essentially moral nihilists. What they call democracy is for them simply the best vehicle for advancing their own power.

Peaceful relations among individuals, groups, and peoples require a robust and resilient check on human arrogance and self-absorption. Besides humility and moderation, genuine mutual respect among cultures presupposes a sense of shared higher humanity and a recognition that this higher humanity can manifest itself in diverse ways.

The school of political theory to which Allan Bloom belongs has been examined here not because it is intrinsically important philosophically but because it has a large following and strongly influences American political and journalistic circles. The school attacks what it calls "historicism." By that term it means any doctrine that sees value preferences as historically conditioned or that attributes normative authority to historically derived practices and identities. Only standards formulated by reason, apart from history, have validity, according to Straussianism. One target of the antihistoricist attacks has been Edmund Burke, who is a critic of what he terms "abstract" and "metaphysical" reason as sources of social order. Burke draws attention to man's indebtedness to his ancestors, to the accumulated wisdom that he calls the "bank and capital of nations and of ages." Burke believes that reason should be historically rooted and informed and that the higher purposes of civilization must always be adjusted to time and place. On that account, the antihistoricist Leo Strauss criticizes Burke as a historical relativist who disparages reason. Strauss chastises him for not accepting that society should be formed according to a single rational design. Strauss rejects Burke's emphasis on the importance of adapting to historical circumstances and especially his respect for historical particularity, for "individuality"—a respect that seems to

Strauss incompatible with a belief in universality. Only a rational and universally valid plan—one that is "simply right"—should command respect, Strauss believes. Not surprisingly, Straussian antihistoricism is a major source of inspiration for many of the new Jacobins, some of whom put a thin veneer of Platonism on a democratist ideology. It is appropriate to add that Strauss's thought contains elements that are not quite as incongruous with the philosophical position taken in this book and that he probably would have been critical of many writers today who think that they are applying his ideas.[11]

In these pages a much different view of universality and particularity has been suggested, and it will be explained at considerable length. There are reasons to be troubled by a theory of universalism that fails to recognize the intimate connection between universality and particularity or understand that universality may become historically concrete. Abstract universalism knowingly or unknowingly drives genuine universality from the world in which we live. It replaces universality with abstract "principles," whose attempted implementation easily results in tyranny and other inhumanity.

11. Burke, *Reflections on the Revolution*, 76. Strauss's antihistorical thinking permeates his most widely read book, *Natural Right and History* (Chicago: University of Chicago Press, 1953). Its section on Burke, pp. 294–323, is philosophically awkward and contains plain inaccuracies. His use of sources is also careless and tendentious. Cf. Joseph Baldacchino, "The Value-Centered Historicism of Edmund Burke," *Modern Age* vol. 27, no. 2 (spring 1983); also available at <www.nhinet.org/burke.htm>.

CHAPTER SEVEN

The Attack on History

The new Jacobinism is but one example in the Western world of a reaction against the moral relativism or nihilism of modern positivism and, more recently, of postmodernism. A sizable number of intellectuals in the West have sought to reaffirm universality, in ethics as well as in epistemology and aesthetics. The questioning of the dominant academic relativism and nihilism might suggest intellectual ferment and conditions favorable for a much-needed philosophical revitalization, but the new interest in universality may be less a sign of intellectual deepening than of ideological fashion. The assertions of moral obligation typically lack philosophical stringency, and they run in many directions. Universal "values" or "rights" are cited in support of traditional Christian norms of personal conduct, but also of "alternative lifestyles," in support of private property and social differentiation, but also of egalitarian reconstruction of society, in support of minimal government, but also of socialist collectivism, and so on. The notion of a higher morality is perhaps most widely identified with a sentimental ethic of "compassion" and "sensitivity," which is usually associated with a preference for government-sponsored welfare measures and, among the most ambitious moralists, for benevolent political intercession abroad in behalf of unfortunate peoples. As discussed in the previous chapter, a common brand of universalism declares "democracy" to be the goal for all societies and buttresses this claim with Jacobin-sounding appeals to "human rights." The language of ethical obligation frequently looks like a gloss on political or other personal preferences for which the particular advocate would like to claim universal sanction.

Affirmations of "universal values," "moral principles," "rights," and the like must consequently be approached with suspicion. But the spread of philosophically dubious claims must not deter a serious reconsideration of the meaning of universality. Rethinking the relationship between universality and historical particularity may be a *sine qua non* for the revitalization of Western thought and may be an aid to similar efforts in other parts of the world.

The continuing purpose here is to define an approach to ethical and other universality that differs markedly from most contemporary notions of moral right, be they philosophically earnest or more ideological. An understanding of universality is being developed that takes full account of the frequent tension between universality and particularity but that also stresses their interdependence and integral connection whenever goodness, truth, or beauty are being realized. This understanding forms part of what the author calls value-centered historicism, which affirms universality while recognizing life's inescapable historicity.

A new conception of universality is needed for many, and varied, reasons. In epistemology, abstract universalist reifications and rigidities stand in the way of a faithful account of the dynamics of actual human knowing. In aesthetics, static, mimetic notions of beauty are not sufficiently sensitive to what is contributed by human creativity and the distinctiveness of artistic visions. In ethics, abstract moral absolutism generates a blueprint approach to the moral life and a weak sense of the variability and actual moral opportunities of human existence. As in the case of the French Jacobins and their descendants, such an approach easily turns putative moral principles into moralistic tyranny. More generally, abstract moral universalism creates a gulf between philosophical propositions and concrete human experience. It does not well prepare the individual for embodying universality in particular actions. This kind of universalism tends to lose the substance of morality in merely abstract considerations of "virtue," "good," "justice," and "rights." Engaging in intricate and protracted discussion to find just the right formulations or to come up with just the right casuistic application of "universal principles" comes to seem more significant than actually improving self or undertaking concrete good actions.

Because this book defends universality, some may regard it as presenting a "metaphysical" argument, but the word *metaphysical* has many meanings. If by that term is meant attempts to ascertain a reality that is not actually or potentially a part of human experience, the argument of this book is not metaphysical. Value-centered historicism makes no claim to knowing what lies beyond consciousness. As understood here, universality can be said to be transcendent in that the particulars of goodness, truth, or beauty in which it manifests itself in human experience never exhaust their source, and in that it finds ever new expressions; but it is not transcendent, if by that term is meant that there is a fundamental discrepancy or discontinuity between the source of value and the immanent world. Such radical transcendence is postulated, for example, by the theologian Karl Barth, who refers to God as "wholly other," and the philosopher-historian Eric Voegelin, who insists that the Divine Ground of being is wholly beyond the world and that attempts to immanentize it are signs of egotistical self-aggrandizement, "egophanic revolt." In value-centered historicism, what may be called the transcendent has an intimate connection, positive or negative, with immanence. Transcendence becomes progressively known through the special kind of experience in which it assumes concrete shape. This understanding of normative reality has little to do with a metaphysics that claims to know a reality entirely beyond human experience. Though philosophy has to admit the possibility of such reality, it has little use for intellectual abstractions that have been formulated apart from life as actually lived by human beings or that extrapolate extravagantly from what is known in experience.

Mankind is always trying to expand the limits of consciousness and to grasp more fully a dimly sensed Beyond. Where philosophy begins to lose its footing, intuition takes over. Intuition can be merely romantic and idiosyncratic, but sometimes it sees more deeply than reason. It may, by reorienting thought and action, cause an expansion of the range of verifiable human experience, which means an expansion also of the field for rational-philosophical inquiry. Rooted as it is in the experiential world in which human beings act, philosophy can help distinguish between religious intuition born of good conduct, humility, and balance and allegedly religious intuition full of imaginative excess and moral conceit.[1]

Value-centered historicism unqualifiedly embraces the historicity of human existence. Everything we do, think, and imagine has a history and is affected by that history. Individuals are made unique by their histories. They view and approach life differently. There is an important sense in which no two persons can act in a practical situation, view a painting, or read a philosophical text in the same way. This insight has been available for many generations. It is a component of German and Italian historicism. It was expressed with special clarity and penetration in the twentieth century by Benedetto Croce. Only persons unfamiliar with the historicist strain in modern Western philosophy could think that we are indebted for this idea to postmodernism. The latter has merely taken it to a frivolous extreme by assuming that historicity is incompatible with universality. Both ahistorical universalists of the Greek variety and postmodernist nihilists mistakenly assume that if we are restricted to history there can be no common human ground, no center of values. The classical abstractionists try to escape from history, which they say has no meaning, to a postulated sphere of disembodied universals. The postmodernists immerse themselves in history, from which they try to exclude what is in fact indistinguishable from it, a power that keeps particularity and diversity from shattering into meaninglessness. Both groups are unable to grasp the idea that particularity and universality might actually coexist, cooperate as well as be in conflict. Value-centered historicism explains the good, the true, and the beautiful as a *synthesis* of universality and particularity. What seems to many philosophers to be theoretically inconceivable is a fact of human experience.

The historicism of this book applies to all spheres of human activity, including the search for truth itself. How do we gain philosophical knowledge? In the humanities and social disciplines we do so by abjuring reifying rationality, which forces on us a world whose every

1. For a systematic examination of philosophical rationality and its relation to intuition, see Ryn, *Will, Imagination and Reason.*

component, large or small—thoughts, emotions, acts, images, as well as "physical objects"—is seen as a kind of "thing," distinct and in its own place. That kind of abstract rationality is useful in natural science and mathematics but has been inappropriately applied to human self-understanding. Genuinely philosophical reason, by contrast, scrutinizes the distinctively human sphere from within actual, concrete experience. It tries to understand *life,* which is a nonmechanistic dynamic of universality and particularity in simultaneous tension and union, a dialectic. What pseudorationality asserts to be impossible philosophical reason can faithfully observe and understand because it, too, is dialectical.[2]

The habit of treating the phenomena of human consciousness as solids of some sort has long plagued Western thought. The mind has been allowed to chop living wholes of experience into pieces for the purpose of analyzing and classifying them, as if they had no inner, organic connection. According to this rather mechanistic and bureaucratic approach to knowledge, a phenomenon cannot both be and not be something at the same time. It must be itself and nothing else. Anything else would be an irrational muddle. Most especially, something particular cannot also be universal. It has to be either "this" or "that." Such thinking excludes the possibility of synthesis by definition. This kind of thinking might, without polemical intent, be called "blockheadedness." This is the mind-set that turns consciousness into building blocks. All people in the Western world are prone, more or less, to this reification of life, for it is an old and deeply ingrained practice.

The long history of abstractionism includes even Aristotle, who was in some other respects a very wise man. He insisted on the logical principle of identity or noncontradiction expressed as "A is A and not non-A." Thinking that did not conform to that principle would, he thought, have to be some kind of confused blur. But in his logic, Aristotle neglected what elsewhere he took for granted, that life is always becoming, changing into something else. He did not consider that a

---

2. The historical and dialectical nature of philosophical reason, is explained in Ryn, *Will, Imagination and Reason,* esp. chs. 4–7.

phenomenon changing into something else cannot be simply "this" and not also "that." Thought, for example, that has not culminated in omniscience is still striving for deeper insight and greater clarity. It has achieved no definitive Truth but is trying to become more truthful. In that situation ideas do not yet have full identity with themselves. This is the permanent intellectual condition of mankind. Even the most profound philosopher always has more work to do; not even the insights about which he is the most confident are conclusive. He knows that they will require elucidation *ad infinitum*. That his thinking thus falls far short of omniscience does not mean that it must be incoherent. It may be both profound and coherent. The good philosopher both knows and does not know the truth at the same time. It is his human predicament never to be quite certain which is which. His work continues. He lives in a state of partial enlightenment in which no thought, outside of the sphere of empty mathematical abstractions, ever achieves perfect self-identity. Hence none of his ideas can be said to conform to the formula, "A is A and not non-A," which is the formula of conceptual self-identity. This formula does not describe the dialectical reality of truth-seeking, of knowing and not knowing at the same time. Identitarian logic is the logic for what is lifeless and abstract. This part of Aristotle's philosophy connects him with modern symbolic logic and analytic philosophy, a type of thought with whose assumptions his work otherwise has little in common. This abstract, formalistic logic does not describe how we actually think; it attributes to the phenomena of human life, including thoughts themselves, a static, thinglike quality that they do not have in actual thinking. Real thought follows a different logic. It is itself constituted by the union and tension of universality and particularity, and it tries conceptually to express human self-experience as it truly is—dynamic, dialectical, living.

What has just been said in criticism of "blockheadedness" and about the dialectical nature of truth can equally well be said about goodness or beauty. Particular instances of either good or beauty are not morally or aesthetically pure specimens of their inspiring values. They, too, represent a straining toward the fuller realization of human potential. They both are and are not complete. The same is true for human life in general, including people of the greatest nobility and refinement. Life can be a striving for, but never the achievement of, perfection. Perfection is an unreal abstraction. It would mean the absence of obstacles and challenges, the end of striving, the cessation of life. Particular persons are always to some extent in movement toward a different condition. A certain person can be said to both be and not be really human. He may be highly civilized and respected for it by others, yet also not quite fully human in that infinite progress is possible toward realizing the higher potential of a human life. A musical composition or a painting taking shape both are and are not a composition or a painting. They are becoming what they are more or less dimly intended to be. In a sense they already exist in the minds of the artists as visions to be realized, or in their unfinished works, but they are also unfinished until the artists have given them their final concrete, aesthetical form. And even when completed they do not exhaust their subject and inspiring value.

A useful step in rethinking the relationship between universality and particularity may be to consider the conflict in the modern Western world between two broad streams of thought concerning that subject. Briefly reviewing these seemingly irreconcilable orientations will help focus attention on the crux of the philosophical matter and help explain the meaning of value-centered historicism. We may restate, extend, and further elucidate earlier reasoning by formulating and defending a thesis: that we should look for universality, not in abstract theoretical "principles" or other ahistorical judgment or vision, but in concrete experience; that normative authority, in so far as it exists for man, makes itself felt in historical particularity, the kind of particularity that gives expression to universality. That such a thesis will strike many as strange, even as a contradiction in terms, shows the pressing need for rethinking the subject. Widespread and deeply rooted habits of dealing with the problem of universality and particularity are stifling philosophical renewal.

The term *universality* has been used here and will be used in what follows to indicate normative structures that invest existence with a higher and enduring significance. But the term may also refer to human life more broadly and point to its salient, recurring, inescapable elements, whether conducive to or destructive of higher values. Universality in the second sense has connotations similar to "the nature of the human condition" or "what life is really like." While the emphasis in this discussion is on universality as normative, that meaning will be found, in the reconstituted understanding here advanced, to be closely intertwined with the second meaning. The reason is that what orders human existence is a power within the ordinary, everyday world of mankind; to realize universal values human beings must overcome obstacles, rise to demanding challenges, and adjust to their own limitations. The context will have to show when this book is emphasizing one or the other of the two meanings of universality. A similar double meaning can be carried by the word *reality*. That term, too, may be used to indicate what completes and gives value to life, but it can also refer more generally to elements that are always present in human existence, good or bad. The argument of this book is directed against the artificial separation of normative universality from "life as it is." One objective is to demonstrate that universal good, conceived as wholly independent of what counteracts it in the world, is a highly questionable and potentially pernicious abstraction.

To those in the modern world who reject the idea of moral universality, the great diversity of views regarding the content of moral good now and throughout history confirms the truth of moral nihilism or relativism. Not only the differences between cultures, they say, but the wide range of beliefs within each belie the existence of any single standard of good. The proliferation of beliefs and lifestyles in modern Western society signifies a welcome abandonment of outdated, static notions of morality.

Liberalism and derivative currents have argued for the need for "pluralism" and individual freedom in setting goals for life. Ethical preferences must not be imposed from without. In maintaining the necessary public order it is essential that the consent of those affected be obtained. The evolving consensus regarding society's general direction and the limits of personal freedom should always be open to revision. These liberal ideas are by no means incompatible with the position being developed here; as joined and adjusted to the notion of universality they become indistinguishable from it. Most of the time, however, liberals today take them in the opposite direction. Plural-ism, for example, is seen as appropriate because there is no universal standard with reference to which a moral consensus might evolve that deserves general respect. There are only subjective preferences. Individuals have to be permitted to live just as they choose, short of interfering with the rights of others to do the same.

Among today's defenders of a higher morality many see thinking of this type as representing an inherently deficient "modernity" or "liberalism." To recover a sense of the universal an earlier mode of thought, classical or Christian, must be revived. Study of Plato and Aristotle is often recommended as providing the proper foundation for understanding ethical right. Philosophical leanings of that kind create profound unease among those who assume the inescapable subjectivity of human likes and dislikes and think of social and political order in terms of social contract or merely pragmatic consensus. To relativists and nihilists, a resurgence of interest in universality means a return to a distasteful moral absolutism and a preference for political authori-tarianism. Accepting a transcendent source of moral order seems to them tantamount to discounting or ignoring personal individuality and the variability of circumstance. Many who profess belief in uni-versality today, such as the Straussians, confirm these suspicions by placing their own concern for moral right in opposition to a concern for the particularity, diversity, and changeability of human existence. To emphasize the historical nature of life, they assert, is to undermine a proper regard for universality. Historically evolved convention could be conducive to good in particular cases, they admit, but tradition as such carries no moral and intellectual authority. The ultimate stan-dard of right must be independent of historically derived beliefs and conditions. How else could the shifting particularities of history be assessed?

Plato places the standard of good beyond what he takes to be the historical flux. He associates the universal with overcoming the world of change and particularity. The highest good is lasting and unchang-ing. Against the dispersion of the Many stands the ordering tran-scendent One. Platonic philosophy contrasts sharply with intellectual currents of the type already mentioned that have asserted particularity and subjectivity to the neglect of universality. The latter emphasis has assumed many different forms—Lockean, romantic, existentialist, postmodern, and so on. In proportion as individualism and pluralism have shed the lingering moral and other prejudices of the older Western tradition, they have tended to extremes of subjectivism. It is perhaps not surprising that thinkers who react against those excesses and to a perceived threat to social order should take an interest in Greek philosophy with its strong affirmation of universality and social cohesion, but the return to premodern sources is usually a detour around the deeper philosophical challenges of modernity. Specifically, this response to subjectivism shows unwillingness or inability to do justice to the historical consciousness and the notion of the concrete universal, achievements in some respects anticipated by Vico but pioneered by German philosophy and revised and extended in important ways in the twentieth century by Benedetto Croce.

Criticisms of historicist philosophy in the name of universal values and truths ordinarily show a fumbling or wholly inadequate grasp of its more fruitful ideas. Sometimes these criticisms betray an outright failure to recognize the possibility of synthesis between universality and particularity. Leo Strauss, for example, is led by his classically inspired conception of reason and natural right to a reductionistic and simplistic view of historicism. He writes: "The historical school asserted that the local and the temporal have a higher value than the universal. . . . By denying the significance, if not the existence, of universal norms, the historical school destroyed the only solid basis of all efforts to transcend the actual."[3] This summary of the meaning of historicism is arbitrary and misleading; it is rather how historicism appears to a mind poorly equipped because of its abstractionist notion of universality to do justice to a different conception of universality. Strauss's depiction may describe some particular representatives of the historical school, but he ignores, because he fails to grasp, the possibility of concrete universality. Contrary to Strauss's interpretation, a historicist appreci-

3. Strauss, *Natural Right and History,* 14–15. For a critique of Strauss's abstract and static conception of reason and natural right, see Ryn, *Will, Imagination and Reason,* esp. ch. 7; and Claes G. Ryn, "History and the Moral Order," in *The Ethical Dimension of Political Life,* ed. Francis Canavan (Durham: Duke University Press, 1983).

ation for the local, the temporal, and the circumstantial need not be the same as demoting or abandoning the universal. On the contrary, such an appreciation is fully compatible with, may indeed arise from, a recognition that moral, aesthetical, and logical universality are infinitely adaptable and can invest historical particularity with a special significance so that particularity becomes a vehicle for the universal.

Many universalists leave the impression that philosophical modernity as a whole should be rejected in favor of ancient thinkers like Plato and Aristotle, or a Christian thinker like Thomas Aquinas. This group includes many Straussians but also a thinker like Alasdair MacIntyre. At the same time, their apparent antimodernism does not necessarily stop them, especially not the Straussians, from selectively reading modern ideas that they like back into the allegedly authoritative authors of the past, as when ideologically willful thinkers, Allan Bloom among them, portray Plato as a democrat in disguise.

Is there then little justification for the modern emphasis on individual freedom and pluralism? Was the relationship between universality and particularity adequately understood by premodern thought? In order to move closer to the universal, do we, as is argued by some today, need to shun individuality and particularity as far as possible? Is the universal good untainted by our historical existence? Does reality lie somewhere else? These questions have already been answered in the negative in earlier chapters of this book and are reiterated here merely to indicate the philosophical context in which some thinkers opt for an ahistorical type of reasoning.

One widely read political thinker who admires the "ancients" for having an ahistorical notion of universality is Strauss. His own way of dealing with universality and particularity, though of limited philosophical importance, may illustrate a contemporary approach to the issue that is not confined to him or his followers. Strauss cannot conceive of the possibility that being attentive to individuality and particularity could be reconciled with a proper concern for universality. This excluded possibility explains his ambivalence about Edmund Burke. On the one hand, Strauss regards Burke's practical conservatism as being in "full agreement" with classical thought. But, on the other hand, Burke's thought represents a new historical emphasis that somehow

connects particularity, diversity, and circumstance with what is normative. The association of universality with historical individuality helps
prepare the way for philosophically disastrous developments, Strauss
asserts. These destroy the ancient concentration on what is right in
itself regardless of historical circumstances. The central issue is formulated by Strauss as follows: "The quarrel between the ancients and the
moderns concerns eventually, and perhaps even from the beginning,
the status of 'individuality.' "[4] Good philosophy, he believes, is not interested in individuality, in historical particulars, which are transitory
and forever changing, but in universality, which is permanent and
unchanging and exists apart from history.

Many who claim to defend universal values regard historicism as
a great threat because it stresses the inescapably historical nature of
human existence. Historicism sees a need for moral and other judgment to be informed by and adjusted to experience and individual
circumstances, a requirement that is said by the antihistoricists to undermine universal standards. Before considering the plausibility of this
criticism it should be noted that historicism has been defined in different ways over the years and that the connotations of the term vary
considerably depending on who is using it. In postmodernism, for
example, the term does imply a denial of all universality. In these circles the historicity of human existence is widely regarded as proof of
the impossibility of shared meaning or continuity. The postmodernist
view of historicity confirms the antihistoricist fear that emphasizing
the historical dimension of human existence undermines the recognition of universality. In this book, "historicism" refers broadly to the
historical sense that emerged in eighteenth-century Europe and became a powerful philosophical force in nineteenth-century German
philosophy—what has been called *Historismus*. Though this kind of
thinking assumed many forms, some of them not very fruitful, it did
in its general trend permanently change the Western mind. This philosophical trend has sometimes lost momentum due to both competing
influences and its own various derailments and potential weaknesses,
but it has, even though its meaning and import are still not fully

4. Strauss, *Natural Right and History,* 318, 323.

recognized or understood, become an integral part of the Western mind, which is evident not least from critiques of the historical consciousness. The historicist movement received a major philosophical boost in the twentieth century through the work of Croce.

As used in these pages, then, the term *historicism* does not encompass all the special meanings that it has had in the past or happens to have in current postmodernist discussion. The term refers generally to the recognition that the present is what it is because of its history and that all human self-understanding is historical and historically conditioned. To study man more than superficially is to study what brought him to the present point. Those who live now are in a sense as old as the human race. Most individuals, when exploring their own selves, that is, their own humanity, do not delve very deeply into their past to try to bring it into more conscious awareness, but truly understanding self involves tracing its history, the marks left on it by other human beings, many or most of them from previous generations, as well as by personal action. For example, as a beginning student of Western political philosophy starts reading the classics of the discipline he discovers that he already has in him some of Plato, Aristotle, Cicero, St. Augustine, and other influential thinkers in the distant past, even though he has not previously studied them or even heard all of their names. Reading their works helps him understand what lies behind some of his already-formed inclinations. It helps him understand who he is, as an individual and a member of the human race. These thinkers were a part of his life even before he began studying them. Their ideas had seeped into his consciousness from the culture that nurtured him all his life. Even the part of his self that is in opposition to what they represent testifies to their presence.

This process of self-discovery is not conducted from a vantage point outside of history where everything can be more clearly seen. The attempt to understand life better is made from within the only source of evidence that man has available to him, his own experience, which is indistinguishable from the past that shaped it. The desire for a deeper knowledge of history is inspired by present confusion and most of all by the need to act in the present with understanding. In that sense all attempts to know are conditioned by a historical situation. To know oneself and one's circumstances better requires understanding how they came to be what they are.

The philosophical stance here being developed is called value-centered historicism because it takes the historical consciousness to be awareness in part of the presence and record of the good, the true, and the beautiful. The central philosophical objective of this book is to demonstrate that a full appreciation of the historicity of human existence is wholly congruent with a belief in universality. In fact, the kind of universalism that is philosophically wholly resistant to historicism asserts a purely abstract, artificial, and ultimately inhumane standard of life.

According to antihistoricist defenders of universality, letting historical considerations affect the determination of moral right is to slide into relativism and nihilism. History belongs to the flux of change, they claim, and is inherently incapable of providing moral direction. The sole source of authoritative guidance is reason, they insist. Strauss and his followers set up a sharp dichotomy between historically derived or conditioned standards and what is discovered by reason in "nature." The following passage not only distinguishes between the two but stresses their opposition:

> The conventional is antithetical to the natural in the way that a standard of conduct founded only on the agreement of men is contrary *in its essence* to a standard that would arise out of the nature of men and things independently of human agreements. The standards that men establish are of course artificial.

To be "respectful of the conventional, the artificial, and the traditional" is "to that extent to abjure nature and reason."[5] Attributing any authority to a traditional consensus indicates disregard for a universal source of judgment. Formulas like these, oft-repeated though they be in some intellectual circles, reveal a philosophically retrograde, even

---

5. Joseph Cropsey, *Political Philosophy and the Issues of Politics* (Chicago: University of Chicago Press, 1977), 117–18 (emphasis added).

simplistic understanding of the relationship between universality and particularity.[6]

Under the partly unconscious influence of modern rationalism, antihistoricist admirers of Greek philosophy conceive of universality in a more radically ahistorical manner than was possible in the ancient world. Despite Plato's and Aristotle's stated epistemological assumption that there can be no knowledge of what is particular, the two thinkers, especially the latter, give much attention to the concrete in their philosophical practice. The meaning of Plato's dialogues is inseparable from the particular personalities and states of soul that are vividly described in them. Socrates, the individual—person and philosopher in one—comes immediately to mind. Plato is a literary artist as well as a philosopher more strictly speaking and manages to convey much of his view of life through the portrayal of personages, events, and states of experience. The concrete *embodies* meaning. Aristotle's reasoning in the *Nicomachean Ethics* assumes some familiarity on the part of the reader with the experiential referents of various terms. We must reason from what is personally known to us. Aristotle's studies of

---

6. Straussians sometimes stress the importance of distinguishing between two types of writing, including writing by their own number: "Exoteric" writing is addressed to the unenlightened and may feign respect for convention for prudential reasons; "esoteric," "secret" writing reveals the truth (which may turn out to be nihilistic) to a few enlightened minds. A convenient consequence of this distinction is that criticism of texts that the Straussians consider authoritative can always be dismissed as seizing upon the mere surface of ideas, whereas the real meaning of the work is incontestable, although naturally beyond the grasp of the critic. Here arises an opportunity for philosophical self-contradiction and vacillation to present themselves as high sophistication and cleverness.

That writers have often felt the need to conceal their innermost thoughts from the powers-that-be is indubitable and worthy of study; yet a claim by a school of thought that its real foundation is to be found in secret writing is actually a damning self-indictment. Serious thinkers know that in philosophy central questions are highly complex and linked to other questions in involved and subtle relationships. To elucidate them is exceedingly difficult even when it can be done in an entirely open, systematic, protracted manner. Whole books of such explicit, elaborate writing are sometimes required to achieve the needed clarity. The suggestion that insights of any consequence, as distinguished from hints and loosely formulated ideas, could be smuggled into other writing "between the lines" calls into question the claim of the genre of secret writing to be a philosophical enterprise. The deceit may be self-deceiving.

a wide range of concrete materials, such as the specifics of a large number of city-state "constitutions," or "regimes," indicate an awareness, however vague, that particularity is in some way knowable and a guide to the universal. This assumed connection between particularity and universality is not adequately accounted for in the classical Western doctrine that knowledge pertains only to universals.

Although the Greek thinkers did think of normative reality as being in some way above and beyond the realm of change, it is anachronistic to attribute to them, particularly Aristotle, a purely ahistorical rationality. They had not conceived of particularity and individuality in the modern sense. They did not possess the self-consciously historical vantage point from which the present is seen as a conspectus and product of the past. They did not use the term *history* as we do. They certainly could not rigorously exclude from their conception of reason something of which they were only dimly aware. The kind of abstract universalism that antihistoricists espouse today presupposes at least a groping modern historical sense that they can at the same time reject.

Those who see in Plato the exponent of purely ahistorical rationality show themselves to be influenced by modern abstractionism. Strauss's followers usually read into the "ancients" ideas derived from the Enlightenment and related philosophical currents. Socrates, for instance, appears as a proto-Enlightenment figure. Plato is believed to have a great deal in common with Jean-Jacques Rousseau, and Aristotle with John Locke, and these modern thinkers, too, are interpreted in the light of even later ideas. One may say about the conception of moral universality associated with this kind of abstractionism that it often bears a greater resemblance to the ideas of the French Enlightenment and the French Revolution than to classical notions of human good.

Great philosophical perspicacity is claimed for the view that ethical and other insights must take form apart from historical considerations, but the antihistoricist association of universality with abstract rationality or other ahistorical contemplation typifies neglect of major philosophical opportunities brought by the last two centuries. Deep-seated prejudices militate against discerning the deeper significance and more promising potentialities of the modern historical consciousness, of the recognition that the present always depends upon and develops the past. These prejudices block a notion of universality that is more attentive to the adaptability of universality to the special and concrete needs of human individuals in diverse and vastly different personal circumstances. Because of its abstract quality, the universality that the antihistoricists assert never quite connects with the uniqueness of particular situations and the life of practice but is confined to the realm of abstract theorizing.

Before turning to an approach to universality and particularity that recognizes their potential compatibility and mutual dependence, it should be added and emphasized that a reluctance to consider the historicity of human existence or to be tied in other ways to the concrete is not restricted to forms of abstract rationality. Avoidance of the here and now of actual human experience always involves interplay between the intellect and the imagination. A desire to set aside the historical world sometimes marks the imagination of poets, painters, or composers, but a similar desire may affect the imagination of writers of treatises. Doctrines that are highly intellectualistic in appearance may, upon closer examination, turn out to be animated by dreamy imaginative vision.

Imaginative escape from what is disappointing in real life has always existed, but the last two hundred years provide a particularly rich flora of what may be called the imagination of daydreaming. The individual drifts away into a sphere of his own creation that has little in common with the concrete needs and opportunities of actual life and that is felt to be so much more satisfying. While indulging this quality of imagination the person does not have to face the annoying obstacles and burdensome responsibilities of the existing world. This type of imagination may be contrasted with other forms, artistic or otherwise, which, though they create or contemplate possibilities, personages, and events that do not exist historically, are nevertheless permeated by a strong sense of realism and limits, a sense of what life could and could not become. The imagination of escape expresses a longing to be somewhere else, to enjoy vastly more fulfilling conditions than the present world can offer. At the extreme, this longing becomes a complete rejection of that world. The specifics of this type of dreaming may vary greatly from person to person. It may, for example, revel in nostalgia for the past, pastoral reveries, dreams of free erotic love, or visions of society virtuously transformed. In the last two centuries the imagination of daydreaming has increasingly refused to confine itself to passing flights of fancy. It has built up elaborate visions that are invested by the bearer with greater worth and significance than the world in which we act. For many, this quality of imagination has become a permanent accompaniment of daily life, a source of chronic grievance against things as they are. The individual dwells more and more in his favorite dream and uses it as a model for criticizing an existing world that seems ever more boring, nay, intolerable.[7]

The imagination of daydreaming is ahistorical or antihistorical not just in the sense that, as imagination, it is intuitive vision and not perception of historical reality. It is ahistorical or antihistorical also in the special sense that it tends to ignore or play down important facts of the human condition as known to living, acting human beings. While this form of avoidance employs and appeals to the imagination, it would be a serious error to view it as unrelated to ways of discounting historical reality that appear to be more rational or scientific. On the contrary, doctrinal or philosophical statements always rest on an underlying preconceptual apprehension of life. They rest on a quality of the imagination, whether evasive or more realistic, which orients the mind of the author. Bacon, Comte, and Marx are examples of individuals who seem wholly enamored of a scientific approach but who are as much dreamers as they are intellectuals. Their way of seeing man and society is powerfully influenced by imaginative visions of a new world. The same is true of ostensibly dry and rationalistic thinkers like John Locke or John Stuart Mill. Indeed, it is appropriate to ask if the deepest attraction of many seemingly rationalistic or scientific

7. For a discussion of the imagination of escape and its relationship to modern moral and social thought and revolutionary ideology, see Claes G. Ryn, "Imaginative Origins of Modernity: Life as Daydream and Nightmare," *Humanitas* vol. 10, no. 2 (1997); also available at <www.nhinet.org/ryn10–2.htm>. The classic and pioneering work on the role of self-deluding forms of the imagination in inspiring a flight from the moral conditions of human existence is Babbitt, *Rousseau and Romanticism*.

doctrines does not lie less in their purely intellectual content than in the intuitive vision of life that they imply and to which they give intellectual expression. Did anyone ever become a socialist by absorbing the strictly technical reasoning of *Das Kapital* or a liberal by similarly absorbing Locke's *Second Treatise*?[8]

If all doctrines receive much of their inspiration, structure, and direction from a certain quality of the imagination and some doctrines are diverted from historical reality by escapist imagination, it is also the case that theories, as theories, can be more or less attuned to actual human experience. Whatever the ultimate source of neglecting or disparaging the historical, philosophical abstractionism of various types more or less deliberately separates itself from the concrete and particular and becomes absorbed into purely theoretical or "ideal" considerations and propositions. The diversity of life holds no interest for it, except as something to be avoided. A precondition for really understanding and appreciating the distinctiveness of cultures, societies, and individuals is rejecting abstractionism and fully embracing the historical consciousness.

8. The relationship between imagination and rationality of different types and the way in which the imagination predisposes reason is discussed at length in Ryn, *Will, Imagination and Reason*. For a careful, amply documented demonstration of how imagination of a certain kind structured and suffused the thinking of an apparently highly rationalistic thinker, see Linda Raeder, *John Stuart Mill and the Religion of Humanity* (Columbia: University of Missouri Press, 2002).

CHAPTER EIGHT

Value-Centered Historicism

The argument of this book is directed against an artificial separation of universality and particularity, a separation that is detrimental to human well-being across the entire range of life. That universality and particularity are frequently in tension—as when particular persons or particular impulses within persons undermine the higher potentialities of life—is not in dispute. What needs to be discussed further is that the universal is not some ahistorical norm without integral connection to the historical world inhabited by human beings. This chapter will develop the idea that it is through concrete particulars that universality manifests itself and becomes more fully known. The idea will be explained partly by showing what it is not.

It may be helpful briefly to indicate a few of the sources for the historicist view propounded here. Among the thinkers who prepared the way for a new, more subtle understanding of the relation of the universal to the particular, Hegel stands out as a groundbreaking figure, though he is partially preceded by Vico in Italy and Burke in England and though his thought has serious flaws. His best insights were much strengthened, expanded, and made more lucid by Benedetto Croce, who is perhaps the greatest technical and systematic philosopher of the twentieth century. Hegelian and neo-Hegelian historicism has sometimes been drawn in very questionable directions—including excessive intellectualization of the human spirit, schematization of history, progressivism, and a monistic-pantheistic blurring of good and evil—but these tendencies can be resisted in favor of developing the more fruitful strains of the same current of ideas. Among the early contributors to the new historical consciousness, Edmund Burke is a central figure. He gave voice to an advanced historical sense before

Hegel, and in some respects he sees more deeply than the German, though he is not a philosopher in the stricter sense of the word. He is an exceptionally perceptive social and political thinker, partly because of his early interest in aesthetics. His understanding of society and the individual as part of an evolving historical whole represents a notable deepening of Western thought and has important implications for all areas of philosophy. Babbitt's notion of the universal as "a oneness that is always changing" is derived partly from Burke, as is his notion of the moral imagination. Burke's strong awareness of man's dependence on and indebtedness to the past is not vitiated by any of the mentioned weaknesses of Hegelian historicism. For example, his humility and awe before the mystery of history that he calls "Providence" have a tenor quite different from that of Hegel's assumption that his own historical consciousness represents the culminating moment in history. By drawing selectively on these and related thinkers and by supplementing and synthesizing them, the idea of universality can be reconstituted into what is here called value-centered historicism.

The emergence of the historical consciousness represents a major advance in Western thought, and modernity, in so far as it incorporates this development, does not have to constitute a radical break with the older Western traditions. Historicism of the type propounded here can be seen as opening up opportunities for reinvigorating and reconstructing important elements of older Western thought and practice and for adapting them to changed moral, cultural, and intellectual circumstances.

Choosing between modern and premodern thought, as if these belonged to distinct intellectual spheres, is not a real possibility. Helpful and necessary as it is for many purposes to classify and label currents of ideas, such differentiations must be understood as creations of convenience and not be mistaken for sharp divisions within concrete reality itself. Actual thought is marked by a perpetual give and take between different points of view and defies the neat boundaries of abstractly conceived categories. Today's partisans for either "modernity" or "premodernity," for example, are themselves products of each. A more recently invented category, "postmodernity," may usefully add to the typology of Western thought for some analytical purposes, but that term, too, suffers from the kind of simplification that must, to a greater or lesser degree, characterize any classificatory scheme of this type.[1] As commonly used, the notion of postmodernity is very fluid, and it assumes a highly eclectic and reductionistic understanding of modernity. In some respects, postmodernity itself looks very much like a variant or mutation of some aspects of "modernity." For example, its elements of Rousseauism and romanticism are prominent. In other respects, a postmodern critique of modernity that avoids the rashness and extremism to which postmodernism is prone can create openings for revisiting some premodern ideas. While recognizing the always pressing need for classifications, definitions, and general terms, it is essential to guard against the danger of reductionism and against rigidly held preconceptions about which ideas belong or do not belong together. Especially in the present historical circumstances, openness to new and perhaps unexpected philosophical combinations and syntheses is in order.

Central classical and Christian insights can be developed and strengthened by drawing on major accomplishments of Western philosophy in the last two and a half centuries. The converse is equally true. Specifically, it is possible to reconcile acceptance of universality with a historicist appreciation for the particularity, diversity, and changeability of human existence. What is here called value-centered historicism refers precisely to the needed reconstitution and synthesis of philosophical elements. In this form of historicism real universality is not separated from the particulars of history; universality is seen as present to human consciousness in concrete form. Ethical universality is at the same time transcendent of historical experience and immanent in it—a statement that is not contradictory but expressive of the

---

1. Croce distinguishes between pragmatic and philosophical concepts. The former are indispensable as tools of practical convenience, but they are not philosophical in the sense of expressing concrete reality. The classifications on which they rest are in a sense arbitrary; these concepts are inherently vague and serve only a limited objective. Only philosophical concepts express actual and enduring structures of life. They do not blur into each other. On this issue, see, in particular, Benedetto Croce, *Logic* (Rome: Laterza, 1908; trans. Douglas Ainslie, London: Macmillan, 1917). Croce's distinction between two types of concepts is discussed and incorporated into a general epistemology in Ryn, *Will, Imagination and Reason*.

dialectical nature of reality. Purely abstract conceptions of universality distort living reality. Babbitt expresses his opposition to what has here been called abstractionism when he writes: "Because one can perceive immediately an element of unity in things, it does not follow that one is justified in establishing a world of essences or entities or 'ideas' above the flux."[2]

More concretely, from what is the emerging understanding of universality different? Modern antihistoricist moralism takes to an extreme a recurring tendency in traditional Western ethics: a failure to engage the concrete texture of day-to-day human life. In political philosophy, for example, such moralism has deemed it dangerous for morality to become too closely associated with an ordinary mundane life that is really unworthy of it and could taint it with impurities. Better for the noble soul to remain aloof.

Plato's moral and political philosophy contains different strains and is not easily categorized, but it offers many telling examples of a disinclination to live in the world as it is. Plato even tries to prove the moral superiority of withdrawing from the ordinary state of politics. In the *Seventh Letter* he vents his personal disgust with participating in actual politics, as distinguished from contemplating ideal propositions. Neglecting the concrete moral opportunities of the world is far from the whole truth about Platonic moral philosophy, and in later Western moral speculation of this inspiration as well that tendency has been mitigated by other factors. Still, a fondness for moral abstractions— "ideals," "principles," "laws"—has tended to divert attention from the needs of actual situations and to create a lack of readiness and ability to act in the here and now.

For example, a case can be made that Platonic political idealism has done little to enhance the moral quality of politics or even to make it more efficient. Machiavelli is one who protests against the old habit of placing moral standards so far from what is actually possible that they, in fact, become distractions from those steps that could actually improve given situations. He points out that the ideal is of no help in looking for actions that might work in the world as it is.

2. Babbitt, *Rousseau and Romanticism*, lxxiii.

His strictures against older political thought for being less interested in "things as they are in real truth" than in dreaming up abstract models for emulation are to some extent infected by dubious motives and an amoral utilitarianism, but he is surely justified in challenging a political moralism that somehow always leaves the politician at a loss in the imperfect, tension-filled and taxing circumstances in which he must act. In spite of its glaring defects, this kind of detached moralism claims credit for being so nobly poised outside the struggle.[3] According to value-centered historicism, in contrast, it is a distinguishing mark of genuine morality to be fully at home in the historical world and to be ready for action in it, although, needless to say, those who try to realize it in action must always strain to resist and overcome that in themselves and in the world that opposes it.

Today's critics of moral relativism and nihilism commonly assert the existence of universal principles whose nobility is supposed to be demonstrated by their distance from imperfect and often distasteful practical reality. Moralism of this type can be seen to be in fact an evasion of concrete moral obligations. Purportedly high ideals, which are "high" precisely in the sense that they put an unpropitious present to shame, are not easily applied to the here and now and therefore tend to become an excuse for inaction. They lend themselves better to unctuous theoretical pronouncements. Croce writes perceptively about antihistoricist moralists that they are "anxious to put morality outside the pale of history, and think to exalt it, so that it can agreeably be reverenced from afar and neglected from near at hand."[4] Behind incorruptible dedication to an imagined pure goodness hides a reluctance to face the real world and an inability to seize moral opportunities actually available in it—an abdication of responsibility that is nevertheless accompanied by self-congratulation.

3. Niccolò Machiavelli, *The Prince* (Harmondsworth: Penguin Books, 1977), 90 (ch. 15). For an analysis and interpretation of the tendency to avoid political reality in Western moral speculation, with special reference to Plato's notion of political virtue, see Claes G. Ryn, "The Politics of Transcendence: The Pretentious Passivity of Platonic Idealism," *Humanitas* vol. 12, no. 2 (1999); also available at <www.nhinet.org/ryn12-2.htm>.

4. Croce, *Story of Liberty,* xv.

Some writers who attempt a return to older Western traditions in social and political thought invoke transcendent spiritual reality and mystical experience.[5] But that reality is often so loosely conceived and so tenuously related to the ordinary, immanent world that its concrete, specific entailments and implications for how to live remain obscure. If the transcendent is not seen as a source for structuring concrete existence but is regarded rather as pulling the person away from the need to assert will, imagination, and reason in the present, this genre falls into the mentioned pattern of pseudovirtuous withdrawal. That type of escape should not be confused with the special and rare kind of otherworldliness known to the religions that was discussed in an earlier chapter. The religious aspiration to holiness involves renunciation of the world in one sense, but also faces up to the concrete obstacles and demands it must confront in the here and now, especially within the person, to move closer to its goal. That kind of striving embodies its aspiration in pragmatic, down-to-earth, realistic conduct, though chiefly in inner action directed at purification of self. What looks dubious in the perspective of value-centered historicism is a very different kind of spirituality, the kind of ethereal piety that disparages the immanent world and casts aspersions on the means necessary to act in that world—compromise, politics, self-assertion, power, economic resources, etc.—and that considers its hands beautifully clean for not wishing to touch such shoddy merchandise.

A failure to connect ethical universality with historical particularity, so that it never has to reveal itself in the concrete and be scrutinized as to its effects, makes it easier for widely divergent proponents of moral virtue to appropriate the high-sounding language of universality. Ethical universality that does not become embodied in specific aspirations leaves its quality and direction obscure. General terms such as "the transcendent" and "the universal" then become so elastic that they can be used to turn merely subjective preferences and spiritual conceit into something worthy of the attention and respect of all mankind.

5. See Ryn, "Politics of Transcendence."

Explaining the coexistence of universality and particularity is complicated in the West by the prevalence of vaguely empirical conceptions of "experience." Experience is usually regarded as derivative of "the senses," a definition which produces an exceedingly narrow notion of what lies within man's concrete and direct apprehension. What is ordinarily called "the senses" represents a simplistic account of the source of human knowing. A vaguely empiricist prejudice associates experience with a mundane, "sensual" reality, whereas "higher values" are thought to belong to some other sphere. It should be made clear that in the historicism advocated here "experience" does not carry these empiricist connotations. The term refers to all of what falls within human consciousness, to the whole range of man's awareness of what it is to be human. Experience includes the facts of morality, religion, politics, economics, art, and knowledge, as apprehended by living, breathing human beings. It includes the special intimations and satisfactions of goodness, truth, and beauty. To be human is to have a consciousness in which the past is moving and in which potentialities for the future are stirring. Experience is not an aggregate of inert phenomena, of "things," as discussed before. Every action has a historical context and can be developed further. Human creativity is forever opening up new possibilities, for good or ill. Hartshorne once said that if philosophy is only about what we are conscious of, it is not about very much. His statement indicates a truncated notion of consciousness. In any case, only that which has entered human experience can be handled with any authority by philosophical reason. The experiential whole of the entirety of human life is more than sufficient to keep philosophy occupied. It is vastly beyond what the reason of any individual can encompass and digest. Even the most profound and knowledgeable philosophers admit their indebtedness to other thinkers and the enormity of the work remaining. It is of course possible that what lies outside of human apprehension is more important than what lies within it, but that which does not in any way become a part of human experience is by definition inaccessible to philosophical scrutiny. That which does enter experience gives philosophy an infinite task.

It should be added that man's self-understanding expands and contracts. Suddenly humanity is able to articulate insight about itself that previously was only fumbling intuition; it gains a deeper, fuller understanding of itself. But sometimes humanity loses knowledge that it had and slips into ignorance in some ways worse than before. Simply maintaining insight already gained, by continually rearticulating and developing it in new circumstances, is by itself a highly demanding challenge.

The particulars of experience can be understood fully only in relation to universality, to that which makes them part of a comprehensible whole in the first place. Without the centering pull of universality, human consciousness would disintegrate. Impulses that are threatening chaos are seen to be such in relation to the potentiality of meaningful life. Yet universality is not a stagnant, unchanging reality, some kind of reprieve from the world of particulars and movement. The alternative to chaos and misery is particularity and movement of a different kind, universality particularized. By its very nature, this alternative is what makes life more fully what it has the potential of becoming. Attempts to make life stand still by tying it to an allegedly unchanging higher norm are destructive of human freedom and creativity, that is, of life itself. They are tyrannical in origin. Universality can be seen as unchanging in the sense that it inspires and promises life of a certain, intrinsically satisfying quality, but it is at the same time always changing in that this quality has to be realized differently depending on the person and the circumstances. Permanence and change, universality and particularity, are aspects of the same higher reality. They condition and need each other. They are unified through synthesis.

The good, the true, and the beautiful are the terms traditionally used in the West to describe the universal values, or imperatives, of human existence. In this book they have also been spoken of together as "the universal" or "universality" in the singular. To this triad should be added what Croce calls "the economical" or "the useful." The latter refers to the efficient employment of means that makes any human activity, whether admirable or contemptible, simply serviceable and coherent. The good, the true, and the beautiful are defined by their respective qualitative ends, but they cannot be realized without being also economical, that is, without the actor, thinker, or artist effectively using the resources available in given circumstances. Since the current discussion deals primarily with universality in general, the ways in which goodness, truth, beauty, and economy differ and interact need not be elaborated. Here the primary aim has been to explain that universality of any kind manifests itself in historical particulars, even as it transcends each new synthesis.[6]

It needs to be explained further how, according to value-centered historicism, history is relevant to the realization of the universal. Let us consider a predicament common to all societies and individuals: that in the quest for a better life they labor under limitations chronic to human nature. All societies and generations have their idiosyncracies, blind spots, partisan preoccupations, areas of special ignorance, and other flaws, which stand in the way of a life more truly worth living. For the sake of that goal they must be constantly mindful of the possible presence of such weaknesses and try to work their way out of them. But how, in the midst of these same limitations, could a society even identify the weaknesses, to say nothing of rising above them?

A society that becomes wholly caught up in the practice, thought, and sensibility of its own time and place will have great difficulty extracting itself from its own deficiencies. It is very different with a society that makes a sustained attempt to familiarize itself with the rich record of what humanity has wrought in the world over the centuries, what Goethe calls the "masses of world history." History speaks of what life may contain—the enviable, the unenviable, the indifferent, and the horrifying. Awareness of the heights of human attainment and of earlier flagrant mistakes can help alert a particular generation or society to its own flaws and to how it might free itself of them. Exposure to history serves as a corrective to the confining biases of time and place and enhances the individual's sense of what has genuine and enduring value.

6. Croce explains "the economical" and its relation to the ethical in *The Philosophy of the Practical* (Rome: Laterza, 1908; trans. Douglas Ainslie, New York: Biblo & Tannen, 1967). The English translation is flawed and sometimes misleading. The forms of universality and their interaction, with particular emphasis on problems of knowledge, are examined in depth in Ryn, *Will, Imagination and Reason.*

In order to improve self or society, it is necessary to envision something better than what currently exists. But here two very different approaches present themselves. One is to cultivate a historically informed sense of what advances might lie in the realm of the possible and to gain insight into the strengths and weaknesses of one's own time through historical comparisons, so that ameliorative efforts are adjusted to real potentialities and to the special needs and opportunities of given historical circumstances. Another possible approach is to define an "ideal" apart from historical considerations and seek its implementation regardless of the situation at hand. In the latter case, what should exist is thought to be obvious from the ideal itself. The "idealist" does not welcome reminders of the actual experience of mankind, full as it is of evidence of the limitations of human beings, or of the restrictions imposed by existing circumstances. He deems these irrelevant to formulating the ideal, which is what it is. To adapt the ideal to a historical situation is to subvert it. It is historical circumstances that should be adapted to the ideal. To have some sort of respect for historically evolved patterns of life is misguided, the idealist contends. The historical is merely accidental and infected by human depravity and is most likely an obstacle to realizing the ideal. Only the latter is worthy of respect. To argue in favor of deference to tradition is for the idealist a form of perverse obstructionism.

Jean-Jacques Rousseau wants to replace existing society with one modeled after his own conception of what should be. In formulating his ideal he proceeds independently of human life as we know it in actual history. His *Second Discourse* offers a history of sorts, written in part to explain the great evils that have befallen humanity and to discredit all existing societies, but it still does not lay claim to historical truth. Rousseau is aware that the facts of actual history might contradict his reasoning, and he treats them as irrelevant to his purpose. "Let us therefore begin," he writes, "by setting all the facts aside, for they do not affect the question." His pseudohistorical account of the original goodness and freedom of man, which has everything to do with justifying the new political order he desires, is prefaced by the statement that "the researches which can be undertaken concerning this subject must not be taken for historical truths, but only for hypothetical and

Value-Centered Historicism

conditional reasonings."[7] Rousseau's reflections about human nature and society are assumed to be no less credible for disregarding concrete historical evidence.

Value-centered historicism sees every reason to admire individuals of exceptional wisdom and virtue and to lean heavily on their advice, but, with Edmund Burke, it also rejects as superficial and dangerous the idea that one could substitute for the slowly accumulating insight and experience of the human race the abstractly and autonomously conceived ideas of a certain individual or group. The ability to improve human life gains from a willingness to learn the lessons of human history. The notion of an ahistorical enlightenment sufficient to guide society ignores not only the intellectual and other limitations of human beings but the extent of the dependence of each individual and generation on preceding generations for the coherence and meaning currently enjoyed. Any approach beyond the superficial to humanity's central problems will take its history very seriously.

Two opposed approaches to improving self or society are thus distinguished by very different assessments of the significance of historical experience. The first resists historical considerations as not germane to formulating the ideal and as raising unwelcome doubts about the possibility or desirability of enacting it. The second—value-centered historicism—distrusts abstract models and looks for opportunities to develop the higher potentialities of actually present historical circumstances.

Value-centered historicism does not assume the inevitability of progress. Such advances as are made by mankind are forever threatened by lapses, retrogressions, and sheer laziness. Since history contains bad as well as good and the potentialities of the present point in many different directions, an ability to discriminate is essential. What needs to be better understood is that there is a vital and necessary connection between the historical sense and the ability to rank possibilities of life. The two are connected because we discern the good, the true, or the beautiful only in concrete experience. Whatever may lie outside of our consciousness is just that, outside, beyond—unavailable for critical

7. Rousseau, *Basic Political Writings, Second Discourse,* 38.

examination. Individuals and peoples are oriented to life's higher possibilities in proportion to their ability to give specific expression to their intuition of universal values. These particulars embody universality, however imperfectly. To the extent that they stir and move the individual soul, life acquires an intrinsically desirable experiential quality.

On the basis of such concrete apprehension, it is also possible to frame philosophical *terms* and *definitions* for the good, the true, and the beautiful, but in value-centered historicism these are not, as they are in ahistorical theorizing, empty ideational abstractions. They give conceptual form to historically realized values.

The normative authority of universal values becomes known to a person in specific instances of moral action, thought, and art. Through them experience is structured and directed in ways that invest life with a special significance. Sometimes, in some individuals, that significance is such as to induce nothing less than deep gratitude, exultation, or awe. If people in general come to share in these values and can thus confirm their intrinsic worth for themselves, new generations can be initiated into the same reality. A civilized heritage is pregnant with new possibilities for realizing the universal. Goodness, truth, and beauty already realized point beyond themselves and their own circumstances.

There is an important sense in which civilization is enriched by building ever new manifestations of universal values into its canons. The way it happens needs to be examined with care. Does civilization progress by means of some kind of accumulation, and, if so, what kind of accumulation is it? What of tradition?

Tradition can be understood in very different ways. Some traditionalists, S. H. Nasr and Tage Lindbom among them, are prone to an essentially static conception. Tradition is for them the transmission of enduring, unchanging, permanent Truth. Tradition is a fixed, divinely ordained order to be kept as safe as possible from the vicissitudes and corrupting influences of history. In the midst of perpetual change, the task of human beings is to strive to conform their lives to the wise prescriptions of the tradition and to protect it against demands for contemporary "relevance." Tradition is something to be perpetuated and possibly extended or elaborated, but not something to be pruned, revised, or reconstituted according to changing historical circumstances. In so far as traditionalism of this kind turns tradition into a norm apart from the mutability of history, it begins to resemble the ahistorical universalism examined earlier, however much the two positions may differ in their moral and other prescriptions. Both of them hypostatize the universal. Both set reified universality in the place of a historically evolving and concrete sense of goodness, truth, and beauty. Although faintly aware of a link between historical experience and normative authority, traditionalism of this type is prone to severing the connection between universality and history. To that extent it becomes another example of the kind of withdrawal from the actual opportunities and challenges of human existence that was discussed above.

The just-mentioned type of traditionalism is, thus, quite different from the view propounded in this book, which is that, though a tradition may contribute greatly to making life truly worth living, the sense of universality associated with such life needs to be continuously rearticulated if it is to be understood, transmitted, and enhanced in new circumstances. Tradition at its best is a living past. It maintains the vitality of its connection with the universal through creativity and change. Depending on their inspiration, creativity and change can assist or undermine the realization of universal values, but they are indispensable to universality shaping man's historical existence. If a capacity for creative adjustment to circumstance is not integral to universality itself, the latter could never be a force in history. It would be unable to make use of the unique moments that constitute human life. To be a reality for man, the universal values that transcend particular situations must employ infinitely variable means. According to value-centered historicism, man participates in the synthesis of the universal and the particular as creative mediator.

The position advocated here is of course also different from the view that, though moral and other conventions structure human life, history has no enduring, transcendent purpose. According to that view, history is a purely immanent, self-contained process in which, through trial and error, there is a slow accumulation of preferences as to how people can live to their own advantage. Ways of life evolve that may be widely accepted but that have no legitimacy beyond the agreement of those who adhere to them. Value-centered historicism contradicts the assertion that there is no source of moral, aesthetical, or intellectual authority other than convention or subjective preference, but, as against an ahistorical notion of universality, it is quick to add that a form of trial and error is fundamental to universality finding its way in history.

A claim that universality has been captured once and for all in a particular tradition or in certain principles is in effect a claim that some people, those who embrace the tradition or the principles, have been granted a reprieve from the human condition, which is to see only dimly into the meaning of life. Universality becomes an exception to the meaninglessness of history. The historical is relevant to what ought to be only in the negative sense that it obscures or interferes with the desirable state.

In the perspective of this book, life appears quite differently. Human existence is enveloped in mystery and is forever moving. Man has great difficulty separating insight from illusion and ignorance and must strain to hold on to the higher meaning that existence may come to possess. Transmitting or deepening a sense of the universal is not a matter of copying a standard already available. It requires constant moral, intellectual, and aesthetical vigilance and fresh articulation of meaning. Goodness, truth, and beauty are in a sense an ever-unfolding discovery. Some historical situations are sharply inimical to the civilizing task. In those circumstances a consciousness of universal values can be kept alive only through exceptional creativity. A traditionalism that attempts a mere repetition of the past loses the experiential reality of the universal in increasingly empty forms and routines.

The weakness of a mere preference for established ways becomes especially acute in a historical era in which widely divergent views of human good have gained strength within the same society and do, in effect, constitute competing traditions. On what grounds does traditionalism then favor one tradition over another? Is it that this tradition is older than the rest? The answer of this book is that the great age of a tradition may create a strong presumption in its favor; ways of life that have been followed by many generations carry more weight and authority than do ones that appear still experimental and untested. Beliefs and practices being very old as well as widely accepted are an indication that humanity has found them conducive to a satisfying life. Yet their age, by itself, does not establish their validity. The crux of the matter is their intrinsic value. Some ways of life are inherently superior to, more deeply rewarding than, others, whatever their age. The difficulty of ranking competing claims is that the criterion for doing so is not some kind of measuring rod set apart from what needs to be assessed. A ready-made standard has not been deposited somewhere, for example, with a particular group of individuals or in a particular tradition. The criterion for discriminating is not in the form of definite "principles" sitting outside of history. It is a sense of general direction forever in need of rearticulation and sharpening. The wisest, most learned, and perceptive representatives of the human race must struggle to maintain it in the midst of history. In recognition of their own fallibility they will do so in humility. They will consult the recurring, considered judgments of the species as a corrective to the self-important opinions of the hour. Only the dogmatic true believer thinks that he has all the answers. What seems to him a clear-cut choice between his own views and those of his competitors is for the more discerning person likely to be a matter of accepting and rejecting elements from each of them. Indeed, perceptive persons may not so much see a need for choosing among old traditions as for recognizing that different traditions may, in spite of their respective weaknesses, serve the same ultimate end in different historical situations.

Formalistic, ahistorical traditionalism leaves mankind's great moral, philosophical, and aesthetical achievements in the past. It tries to live off their reputation and exercise influence in their name. But for these works to acquire genuine authority and move people by their example they have to reveal their intrinsic value in the present. People living now have to make them their own in the sense of accommodating them in their own experience and in the sense of applying their inspiring force to their own circumstances. The old instances of goodness, truth, and beauty must come alive by helping to articulate and expand the individual's own groping sense of universality. They must speak directly to the deeply felt needs of the here and now, take their place among the works of the contemporary world. They can do so on a large scale only if society has somehow managed to prepare its members to absorb their meaning.

The compelling experience in which universality is concretized is at the same time and indistinguishably that of a particular and unique individual and that of humanity in general. To the extent that tradition can connect man with the universal, it is, to underscore a crucial point, a *living* past. In the experience of the particular person, tradition at its best joins past and present in a new, direct apprehension of universality. From within a direct consciousness of enduring higher good, personal and social life can be continuously assessed. Stale habits and conventions can be identified and weeded out in favor of ways that better manifest the universal. Sound tradition is at once dependence on and autonomy from the past.

Tradition is often seen as opposed by radicals and defended by conservatives. But if tradition means the coherence and continuity that of necessity underlie every new creative accomplishment, "radicalism" and "conservatism" are but labels for equally necessary, interdependent strains within a civilizing process that is indistinguishably renewal and preservation. John Dewey, the preeminent American philosopher of pragmatism, does not quite concede the existence of universality as here understood. Rather than a force guiding human creativity, universality is for him a logical "hypothetical." He is especially reluctant to admit moral transcendence. Dewey's philosophy suffers from yet other weaknesses, some of which predispose him to questionable political notions, but he recognizes the great importance of historical continuity. He wholly rejects a radicalism that strikes indiscriminately against inherited ways. He probably would have been a sharp critic of the predominant strains of postmodernism, though one of its leading American figures, Richard Rorty, claims Dewey as a source for his thinking. Dewey is strongly opposed to a generalized suspicion of order. He would have been similarly disinclined to capricious experimentation or "play." He believes that the discoveries made by humanity must not be frivolously jeopardized. Commenting on what he sees as a dangerous element in the vitalist philosophy of Henri

Bergson, Dewey makes an argument that could be read today as a critique of postmodernism:

> A blind creative force is as likely to turn out to be destructive as creative; the vital *élan* may delight in war rather than the laborious arts of civilization, and a mystic splurge be a poor substitute for the detailed work of an intelligence embodied in custom and institution, one which creates by means of flexible continuous contrivances of reorganization.[8]

Though Dewey is usually regarded as a man of the left and as a critic of the past, it should be noted that he does not place his own well-known stress on the need for continual pragmatic experimentation and adjustment to circumstance in blanket opposition to a historical sense of the kind outlined in these pages. In fact, though Dewey would only partially embrace the kind of historicism that is advocated here, the following statement of his own beliefs may actually serve as a summary of value-centered historicism, a summary that, paradoxically, emphasizes its more conservative side:

> We who now live are parts of a humanity that extends into the remote past, a humanity that has interacted with nature. The things of civilization we most prize are not of ourselves. They exist by grace of the doings and sufferings of the continuous human community in which we are a link. Ours is the responsibility of conserving, transmitting, rectifying and expanding the heritage of values we have received that those who come after us may receive it more solid and secure, more widely accessible and more generously shared than we have received it.[9]

8. John Dewey, *Human Nature and Conduct* (New York: Modern Library, 1957), 69. That Dewey's pragmatism is not as inhospitable to universality as is often assumed is evident, for instance, from his recognition of the possibility of a consciousness of "the enduring and comprehending whole" (ibid., 301). Whether, in Dewey, this consciousness tends to become monistic and pantheistic or to assume some less objectionable form is of course an important question.

9. John Dewey, *A Common Faith* (New Haven: Yale University Press, 1968), 87.

This combination of a sense of universality, dependence on the past, and moral responsibility for transmitting and enriching the human heritage connects Dewey's philosophy with the argument presented in this book. Unfortunately, he never systematically articulates this intuition. It remains a mere glimpse of the center of human existence. If he had made more of this strain in his thought, his pragmatism, with its proper concern to give particularity its due, might have become more fully compatible with the kind of historicism and humanism that is being set forth here.

Another factor complicating a rapprochement of this type is that Dewey's notion of the human community is too affected by sentimental humanitarianism. A tendency to romanticize human nature, specifically, to discount man's propensity for evil, makes Dewey underestimate the tension in man between higher and lower potentialities and the importance of moral character as a bulwark and support for civilization. This must be considered a major flaw in his work. Though this book argues for the existence of universality and for the possibility of genuine peace and respect among individuals and peoples, it lends no support to sentimental hopes for nationwide or worldwide community based on fellow feeling. To minimize the weaknesses of human nature only creates false expectations and increases the likelihood that those weaknesses will be unleashed upon the world. Cross-cultural union is possible, but any progress toward that goal is bound to be limited and to depend most heavily on the moral self-discipline and responsibility of the parties involved.

Dewey's optimism affects his political thought, which envisioned ambitious social reconstruction and made him much too optimistic about man's capacity for reasoned, dispassionate discourse. That same flaw is endemic in today's liberal-socialistic debate about the properties and preconditions of the good society. This debate gives little attention to good character as necessary if there is to be a willingness really to listen to arguments.[10] Self-indulgent, self-serving individuals will dismiss ideas that undermine what they take to be in their own

10. On the connection between moral character and openness to truth, see Ryn, *Will, Imagination and Reason.*

interests. Prone to a romantic, indeed, utopian view of human nature, the liberal-socialistic theorists in question suggest that society should and could be guided by rational communal discourse that is broad-based, open-minded, and never-ending, what is often called "deliberative democracy," or "communicative action," in Jürgen Habermas's term. These theorists do not much worry that willfulness and flawed motives will inhibit, not to say preclude, achievement of the kind of selfless, enlightened consensus of which they are dreaming.

Beside Habermas one may turn to John Rawls, Richard Rorty, and John Dryzek for different aspects or versions of the idea that society can be governed according to well-intentioned, inclusive, collective deliberation. The rather airy and diffuse ideal of "deliberative democracy" has an abstractness at odds with the down-to-earth properties of pragmatism, yet Dewey was one of the founders of this way of thinking about society and politics. It combines a Rousseauistic and egalitarian notion of togetherness with an equally questionable expectation of debate that is at once broad-based and enlightened. Partly because of the scientistic tendency in his pragmatism, Dewey also veers in the direction of social engineering.

Considerable agreement between Dewey's thinking and the kind of historicism that is advocated here thus should not obscure that there are also significant tensions between them. Dewey's philosophy as a whole is sharply critical of universalism that looks for reality in essences beyond human experience, but in spite of what looks like promising openings in his thought, he does not, at least not consciously and systematically, pursue the idea that occupies the center of attention in this book, that universality is a union of the transcendent and the immanent. In the passages quoted from Dewey, universality as here conceived only lies implicit.

An attempt has been made in this chapter to break down the old prejudice that deep interest in and respect for particularity is incompatible with a proper concern for universality. A very different view has been presented: that universality is historical potentiality. Although it is potentiality to be realized through human effort, it is not potentiality arbitrarily chosen by human beings. It has its own special authority, a compelling magnetic quality that becomes manifest in each of its articulations. Human creativity at its highest is a response to poten-tiality that commands by its own majesty, urgency, and promise. A person of acute moral, intellectual, or aesthetical sensibility has no choice but to try in his own way to express this intuition of what is needed for human existence to be enriched and elevated. To the extent that actions or works called good or true or beautiful really manifest this higher potentiality, they persuade by their own intrinsic merit. Though they are the creations of individual persons and are as diverse as the personal gifts and circumstances that formed them, they show themselves to be directly or indirectly related to a single centering power. The dimension of that power that seems the most necessary to the realization of its potential is the moral. In the end, the life of the good, the true, and the beautiful depend on moral character.

To be true to life's highest values is thus not the same as to exalt universality and disdain particularity. Only through a union of the two can those values be realized. To explain the meaning of synthesis further more needs to be said about how universality concretizes itself and ennobles historical particularity.

CHAPTER NINE

The Concrete as Normative

To antihistoricist universalism, talk of a possible union of the universal and the particular sounds like an endorsement of whatever is "thrown up" by history. Ahistorical reasoning lacks categories for a relationship that is dynamic and truly mutual. Explaining how historical particularity and universal values can be intimately related, indeed identical, is complicated by the moral, intellectual, and cultural tensions within contemporary Western society and between it and other cultures. These tensions seem to preclude finding universality within history. Postmodernists view the proliferation of competing traditions and beliefs and the emergence of generally unsettled conditions as confirmation of their own moral nihilism or relativism and as salutary victories for diversity. Those who are not willing to give up the idea of universality often react to this erosion of stability and consensus by searching for a firm standard of judgment wholly outside of history. The here and now being problematic and discouraging, they adopt ahistorical philosophical deliberation and abstract "principles" as sources of guidance.

If it is true that today some powerful historical forces are destructive of the higher potentialities of human existence, those developments do not refute the view that when universality reveals itself, it does so only in historical particulars. To stress the historical particularity of the universal is not to deny the need for moral, aesthetical, and philosophical discrimination between historical currents and potentialities. On the contrary, that need is always great, and it calls for powers of discrimination at once subtle and incisive, for the universal and the historical exist in simultaneous synthesis and tension.

But is it not inconsistent to assert, on the one hand, that it is necessary to select among the materials of historical experience, and maintain, on the other hand, that universality, which is surely the source of normative authority, manifests itself in concrete, historical particulars? How could something that is itself historical provide a standard for evaluating history? To ahistorical reasoning such an idea appears blatantly contradictory. It seems to the "blockhead" that the criterion of judgment and the object of judgment, the norm and the phenomenon, must be separate, as a measuring rod is distinct from what it measures. To the proposition that experience itself can be compelling and normative, antihistoricist universalism will object that many different experiences may seem valuable and that individuals disagree on this matter. Since what is felt to be in some way satis-fying varies greatly from person to person, and even from moment to moment in the same person, a criterion external to all particular experience is necessary to determine what is truly noble and ignoble. This objection does contain a kernel of truth, but it springs from a heavy-handed reification of universality and human experience that turns the two into discrete entities without any integral relationship.

Some concrete illustrations may help explain the simultaneous ten-sion between and synthesis of universality and particularity. Consider the very best of upbringing and education. This shaping of the person-ality can be seen as analogous to the moral, intellectual, and aesthetical maturation of a whole generation, or of an entire civilization over the centuries. In the child, an awakening sense of values is articulated and expanded by the norms, personal examples, stories, music, games, clothes, foods, etc. to which the child is exposed. All of these together convey to the young person, in concrete form, a notion of what life is and should be. This is an initiation to the universal as known by civilization. In time, higher values become more fully articulated in experience as absorption of the moral, cultural, and philosophical heritage continues at ever more advanced levels.

It is important to note that the individual does not passively and uncritically adopt externally imposed standards. Universality emerges slowly from a dialectical encounter between the individual's own grop-ing sense of values and the riches of civilization. The maturing young person, especially if sensitive and gifted, begins to notice dissonances between the recommendations of parents, teachers, and other arbiters, on the one side, and his own developing ethical, aesthetical, and intellectual sensibilities, on the other. In childhood the biases of parents may have been an overwhelming influence, but even then an independent sense of values was beginning to make itself felt, and there were limits to how much the taste of the child could be molded.

Initially lacking in subtlety, the sensibility of the young person eventually becomes more acute and versatile as it is challenged and rearticulated by new ethical, aesthetical, and intellectual experiences. Tales, melodies, and rhymes that were enthralling to the child are seen to be infantile when compared to poetry and symphonies that greatly expand the individual's experiential range. An aesthetical sensibility that once thrilled to cartoons and illustrations in children's books begins to cherish the paintings of a Rembrandt.

The curiosity about self and the world, which in childhood was satisfied by greatly simplified explanations, eventually finds expression in the elaborate and systematic study of history, philosophy, and science. At the ethical core of the personality, conscience begins to orient life at an early age, but the person's effort to articulate the sense of moral obligation soon moves far beyond reliance on simple norms once imparted by parents or by children's tales. With an expanding range of practical experience and widening exposure to philosophy and art there can develop a deeper, fuller, and more intricate sense of moral responsibility, one that is marked more and more by moral autonomy in the sense that ethical conscience is personally and acutely felt. Even an individual benefiting from the best possible social and cultural circumstances has to give moral structure to his personality through his own choices. An ethically sensitive and responsible individual will in time learn to detect the impulses of his own self-indulgent ego and will also learn to censure the ego in favor of a gradually discovered and more deeply satisfying quality of life. Moral habits and individual actions that are established and performed in sometimes difficult inner struggle with opposing inclinations do over the years build up a certain character whose experiential tenor gives higher meaning to life. Aristotle uses the word *eudaimonia* (happiness) to speak of that special feeling of simultaneously personal and impersonal satisfaction that results from sustained effort and increasing success in doing what is right rather than what is easy and momentarily pleasurable.

As the individual enters adulthood the influence of parents, teachers, mentors, heroes, and others may weaken. Sometimes the person must object to established authorities because his own sense of the good, the true, and the beautiful deems them deficient. He may feel compelled to challenge them through his own creative expression of the same values. In doing so, the person follows a standard that is in a sense his very own: he knows its authority from personal experience and applies it in his own circumstances by means of his own unique creative gifts. But the standard is at the same time independent and impersonal in that it is felt to be binding not only on the individual but on all human beings. The particular person cannot control its likes and dislikes. It mercilessly censures breaches of its authority. It is to protest the violation or diminution of the standard and to restore or enhance its authority that a truly constructive rebel takes action, be it in morality, art, or philosophy.

Moral agents, thinkers, and artists are free to betray universal values, and they frequently do so, especially if they should be, for example, neurotically disoriented or obsessively attached to some particular degrading desire. But consider the best and most honest among them. They are free to choose but are in a sense also wholly bound to these universal imperatives. They can be at peace with themselves only by trying to honor them in their life and work. If they betray them again and again, they are in a part of themselves painfully aware of an unfulfilled higher potential. The moral actor knows when he is shirking responsibility and soothing himself with excuses. The thinker knows when he is being less than self-critical and slipping past uncomfortable and unsettling ideas, thus relaxing the commitment to truth. The artist knows when he is letting laziness or pandering to popular tastes intrude upon the aesthetic obligation to give only his best. The moral, intellectual, and aesthetic imperatives are intensely private in their demands. The very identity of the particular person is wrapped up in them. But their universality is simultaneously indicated by the fact that the individual cannot dominate them or turn them on and off at will. The person who tries to flee from their authority is left no peace, for he is ignoring something that he senses to be bound up with his own happiness and to be good for its own sake.

Why would a decent person fail to do what he takes to be in his own enduring self-interest? He may simply lack the willpower to resist the desire of the moment or to pursue a higher possibility that will require much energy and time. He may be able temporarily to persuade himself that another course is preferable that promises a satisfaction of its own that is also more immediately available.

As the heritage of humane civilization assists the individual in articulating the moral, intellectual, and aesthetical imperatives of life, that heritage helps make possible not only independence from the tastes of the day but from long-standing convention. Growing internal, personal, firsthand familiarity with the universal puts the person in an ever-better position to test claims of value for himself and to rank particular achievements.

The expansion of the range and depth of experience comes in large part from taking the advice of others and from seeking a corresponding exposure to new possibilities. Some of these possibilities are discovered to offer indispensable new enlightenment or other enrichment. Some offer perspectives or satisfactions that prove to be trivial or merely transitory or to be disappointing in the longer run. Yet other possibilities are found to be immediately fascinating but destructive of a more fundamental harmony of life. A combination of sensibility and strength of will makes it possible for the individual to create and maintain priorities that build insight and enjoyment into the personality. Because of poor guidance, dullness of mind or imagination, or perversity of will, some individuals become listless and disoriented, live for transitory thrills and pleasures, or structure their personalities around some pernicious driving passion. They never escape a sense of the final meaninglessness of existence.

It might be said in response to these arguments that they seem to provide yet more examples of the need for a criterion of good external to experience itself. Without a separate model or norm of some kind, how could it be known whether particular experiences are conducive to or destructive of our higher humanity? It should be granted immediately that qualitative discrimination assumes a standard of some kind. But it is essential not to reify and artificially isolate something that is living and synthesizing. What must be recognized and pondered is that, in the end, we can be truly persuaded of the validity of a value claim only by concrete experience. Intellectual assertions regarding goodness, truth, or beauty must be in some way tested to see whether they keep what they promise, whether they answer to actual possibilities. From the point of view of normative authority, concrete experience is primary, reasoning secondary. It is certainly possible to speak of what is good for man in ideas, but their meaning lies in the articulation of past experience. Theoretical accounts of universal value that cannot in some way appeal to concrete reality will remain unconvincing.

The primacy of direct experience in ascertaining value finds considerable support in Aristotle. Despite the Greek propensity to intellectualize the quest for meaning, Aristotle showed considerable awareness of the normative significance of experience when he stressed the ethical importance of building up sound habits and when he identified the ultimate good for man with happiness. A special feeling of satisfaction, different from mere pleasure, distinguishes the life of ethical action from other kinds. The *Nicomachean Ethics* is a work of philosophy, to be sure. It presents systematic reasoning, definitions, and concepts. It is philosophical despite Aristotle's somewhat bureaucratic cast of mind and sometimes exaggerated fondness for classifications and distinctions, but his treatment of what is morally beneficial or dangerous is, in spite of notable flaws, anchored in the concrete reality of moral action. Such persuasiveness as Aristotle's treatise possesses lies in its ability to connect its terms with the experience of the reader, in this case the experience of moral universality.

What is most needed in order for a person to apprehend universality, then, is not intense theorizing, however helpful good philosophy can be in orienting the individual. The primary need is that the good, the true, and the beautiful should come alive in actual conduct and other experience. How is it known whether this desirable condition is being approached? It is known ultimately by the presence of the special harmony and worth that is intrinsic to the good and cultivated life. *The standard is in that quality of life itself.* It is the nature of the experience that defines "good" and "cultivated."

Philosophical *concepts* that express these qualities are theoretical accounts of what is already known concretely in experience. An adequate philosophy of values is in that sense necessarily historical. The civilized society does indeed need "principles" and rules of conduct, but their formulation is less a philosophical than a pragmatic activity. At their best, they are attempts to guide society's members toward the good, the true, and the beautiful, partly by discouraging a slide in the opposite direction. But principles and rules, however general in formulation and however widely accepted, are not themselves normative ultimates. They are transcended by the living manifestation of universality and should be continually adjusted to it.

It should be reiterated and emphasized that the universal is never exhausted by its particular embodiments. The very best philosophers, artists, and moral actors fall short of perfection—not in the sense of failing to attain a preexisting ideal, "perfection," which is a wholly unhistorical construct, but in the sense that even the greatest human achievements contain potentialities for improvement and development. The universal must be continuously rediscovered and rearticulated. Some tentativeness or uncertainty about how life can be enhanced in particular circumstances is to be expected even of individuals who have gone far in building up a rich and comprehensive experiential basis for judging. They know the great complexity of life and the limits of man's powers. They recognize that the future may disclose possibilities in morality, art, and philosophy that will be, at least in some respects, more truly compelling than the ones they now favor.

The higher purpose of education and upbringing, and of civilization in general, is to foster the moral, aesthetic, and intellectual range that will qualify persons to make informed, authoritative discriminations. This purpose can be, and frequently is, stifled. Imagine a society that confines the development of the person to a very narrow range of experience, a society that makes no effort to expose its members to qualities of life that human beings over the centuries have found most deeply rewarding. Imagine a society that has for some reason become completely absorbed into its own moral, aesthetic and intellectual fashions. People in this society will still experience and value much along the lines of what is made available to them. But they will not be in a position to assess their own preferred enjoyments authoritatively. They may have an appreciation for rock music but lack the preparation for listening to Bach, Mozart, and Beethoven. They may have a large appetite for simple entertainment but be incapable of absorbing Sophocles, Dante, and Shakespeare. They may enjoy snippets of news and the opinions of journalists but have no capacity for advanced historical and philosophical reflection. They may develop the technical and other utilitarian skills necessary for constructing and acquiring creature comforts but know little about satisfying moral and spiritual needs. They may indulge desires for food, drink, sex, and other transitory pleasures but have no understanding of the deeper and lasting satisfaction that the classical and Christian heritage associates with moral self-restraint and other responsibility. Should members of this society feel a gnawing discontent, they will not be able to identify its sources, enclosed as they are within their own ways. They lack critical distance. They are also very ill equipped to assess alternative ways of living—for the same reasons. We may call this society *the idiosyncratic society*. With its own narrow experience and point of view, it knows little about anything else.

If the aim were to improve the condition of such a society, circulating a new doctrine would by itself not go very far. Ideas of classical inspiration, for example, that extol "reason," "justice," "moderation," and "happiness" might attract the curiosity of members of the mentioned society who are vaguely dissatisfied with their present lives, but really grasping and evaluating serious philosophical claims requires much preparation. Formal intellectual brilliance is insufficient, for the claims cannot be understood simply in the abstract. Philosophical ideas of some depth give theoretical expression to a certain body of experience, acquired over a long time through practical and contemplative efforts of a particular kind. People whose own way of life has left them unfamiliar with what the Greeks meant by "aristocratic" character will interpret the various terms of Greek philosophy according to their own experience and consequently distort the words' meaning.

Truly to understand classical or Christian ethical philosophy means to understand it from the standpoint of experience, or, at minimum, to have sufficient familiarity with that experience to be able to enter imaginatively into that ethos. The task of understanding philosophy of this type requires of the hedonistic, whimsical, and ignorant person nothing less than a comprehensive reorientation of the personality through self-discipline and self-education, as assumed by the philosophy, so as to create the range and depth of experience that will begin to qualify the person to evaluate the philosophy.

Some ideas or "ideals" that are said to express universality are only tenuously related to historical experience. As has been discussed, they are alleged to have normative authority precisely because they have been formulated apart from historical considerations. They are said to be valid because they are free of the distraction and the lowering of standards that comes from adjusting to human imperfections. To test ideas like these against real life is to discover that they do not express actual possibilities and that they mask hidden motives. The great distance between the alleged ideal and what historically existing humanity will bear points in some cases to a potential for tyranny.

It now can be more easily seen why the antihistoricist separation of the universal norm from concrete experience is not only epistemologically misguided, but also morally dangerous. To regard universality as a matter of abstract rationality or of historically detached imagination (attitudes that usually go together) makes it easier for various moral preferences to claim universal sanction, for outside of the terms and limits of humanity's actual historical existence the possibilities are endless. The "ideals" need not be plausible, need not have a sense of right grounded in moral character and hence in goodness that is actually achievable. There is no reason, then, to expect that champions of moral universality who claim that its essence exists beyond the world of concrete action should behave more nobly than anybody else; indeed, their insistence that universality is separate from the historical world might lead one to expect the opposite.

What kind of individual is in the best position to judge life's different possibilities? It is one who can compare them to each other because of familiarity with each of them. Needless to say, an individual cannot try out all the leading alternatives in actual conduct before deciding which to choose. For life to have structure and coherence some general orientation has to be favored from the outset, and this is ordinarily the case by virtue of individuals being born into some particular culture. That earliest orientation owes much to parents or other nearby authorities, but it changes as the individual matures. The considered and repeated judgments of past generations are bound to carry considerable weight with a thoughtful person in setting priorities. To some extent, different views of how man should live can be tried out in practice, but they also can be tested by enacting them *in the imagination* on the basis of fair and plentiful evidence. Some of the human range—from good to evil, truth to falsehood, beauty to ugliness—that the individual could not, or would not, actually try out can be understood through historical accounts and the arts. Experience thus acquired expands and embellishes upon insight gained in personal conduct. The task of responsibly and open-mindedly assessing possibilities is made somewhat easier by the fact that the more enduring and well-supported alternatives have large areas of convergence within which in-depth exploration and evaluation is possible. Excursions into less-familiar territory are needed from time to time to test the actual superiority of what has become habitual and well known.

It is possible for society to be such that it facilitates this kind of comparative assessment of the potentialities of life. Imagine a society in which the rising generation is not confined to the popular tastes of the moment but is prepared through upbringing, schooling, and other education to absorb mankind's major achievements in ethics, philosophy, and the arts and to assess these possibilities in relation to each other as well as in relation to more recent claims. This preparation and expansion of human sensibility is characteristic of what may be termed *the versatile society*. This is a society that encourages its inhabitants to live the kind of life that seems to represent the best judgment of the ages but which also leaves individuals freedom to revise, enrich, expand, and deepen this heritage. This is a society in the best possible position to understand the universal. A truly civilized society does, in a sense, know all the weightier, more rewarding possibilities for how to live, just as it knows the weaknesses to which humanity is chronically prone. *Nihil humanum alienum me puto.*[1] It is a versatile society not in the sense that it lacks a sense of purpose and gives every possibility equal respect but in the sense that it is broadly familiar with what life has to offer, good or bad. It is generally acquainted even with what it condemns. It knows a great deal about depravity and evil, not because it encourages them but because they are a propensity of all human beings. Though some individuals manage to limit and control them in themselves, these inclinations are a part of the human condition. They are known to all in personal experience, if not to the same extent. The versatile society is capable of recognizing depravity and evil for what they are, because it knows something about their opposites. One important way in which the opposed potentialities of human life are made familiar to members of the versatile society is through the arts.

By contrast, the idiosyncratic, culturally narrow society previously described knows its own ways, by its own lights, but is incapable of authoritatively assessing those ways, to say nothing of assessing the ways of the very different civilized society about which it has no real knowledge. The idiosyncratic society lacks the experiential range and depth for this task of evaluation. If this society presumes to pass judgment on a quality of life with which it is not familiar, it can only interpret that quality from its own meager point of view, that is, in the experiential terms known to itself, which is to say that it will inevitably distort what it is trying to understand. The more versatile society, on the other hand, has no difficulty understanding the ways of the idiosyncratic society. These fall well within the experience of the civilized society, for the latter contains, besides the quality of life of which it approves, the self-indulgence, impulsiveness, hedonism, superficiality, and ignorance that are never absent from human life. Because of its wider experiential range, the versatile society recognizes the weaknesses of the idiosyncratic society. It tolerates its predilections, if at all, only in tempered, modified form.

The versatile society is generally tolerant, partly to leave sufficient room for improvisation and creativity in the pursuit of a better life, but

---

1. *Lat.* "Nothing human is unfamiliar to me."

it also disapproves or forbids some conduct. The ultimate reason for doing so is not that the conduct is in violation of some abstract norm but that, substantively, it is deeply unworthy of a human being or, in the extreme case, profoundly destructive of what makes life worth living. The laws and other rules of the versatile society are not imitations of some ahistorical norm or divine rulebook; they are attempts to protect an intrinsically rewarding life against intrinsically degrading conduct, degrading not only to the actor but to those affected by his behavior. For example, the versatile society disdains pornography primarily because it is inherently debasing and lecherous and corrosive of the kind of life at which civilization aims. This is but another way of saying that it is immoral and unaesthetic. Only secondarily does this society scorn pornography because it may also have been made illegal.

A word about the natural law tradition in moral philosophy may help explain further the sense in which universality is concrete experience. In so far as the natural law tradition adopts the view that what is ultimately normative in human life is a form of abstract reasoning, it is not very helpful in understanding universality. To that extent it forms part of the highly questionable tendency in the Western world to overintellectualize problems of morality and turn them into questions of thinking or not thinking right. Especially when this kind of philosophizing takes place without the support of a living moral tradition, it tends to lose itself in elaborate abstract definition and casuistry. Moral philosophy of the natural law type is less problematic to the extent that it recognizes the normative primacy of concrete experience and uses "law" or "reason" merely as convenient ways of speaking about structures of life that are inherently satisfying and beneficial. It might be added that much natural law thinking is not chiefly concerned to make fine philosophical distinctions and rather loosely attributes to "reason" an apprehension of value that is really prerational experience.[2]

A truly civilized society does not succumb to self-satisfaction. It

2. The sense in which moral reality is preconceptual is discussed in depth in Ryn, *Will, Imagination and Reason;* see also Croce, *Philosophy of the Practical.*

recognizes that the higher values to which it aspires can be realized differently in different historical circumstances, and it does not consider its own preferences, however well supported, to be incontestable even in its own cultural setting. The complexity, mystery, and changeability of life require the constant rearticulation and renewal of the sense of universality and rule out any final word. The civilized society is open to new possibilities, some of which may challenge long-accepted habits. This openness is motivated by the opposite of nihilistic skepticism. It comes from a desire to protect the good, the true, and the beautiful from rigidity and premature certainty. The openness is fostered by a permanent but necessarily evolving intuition of what makes life truly worth living. It is this awareness of a higher potentiality, kept fresh and vivid by continual reconsideration and questioning, that forms the basis for judging. Authoritative discrimination between high and low falls in the end to the truly mature, gifted, cultivated, and open-minded individuals whose vantage point lets them identify what is low and sordid by its distance from what they know to be intrinsically worth having. To the extent that people in general come to share in this ability to discriminate by absorbing the best that civilization can offer, a sound sense of priorities and proportion will inform social life as a whole.

To object to this view that different traditions claim superiority and that entire cultures disagree on many matters merely draws attention to the high qualifications for judging. Only people of exceptional breadth, depth, and sensibility can compare and rate possibilities of human existence with real authority. The need for a cosmopolitan element in trying to ascertain how universality manifests itself has been discussed earlier. This need only exemplifies the broad preparation required for ranking potentialities of human existence. Conceiving of the standard of good in ahistorical, "idealistic" terms has great appeal over the one here propounded in that it presupposes little in the way of character and general culture. All that is necessary to judge is adherence to a particular doctrine. Great wisdom is made possible on easy terms. Abstractionism thrives and holds particular appeal in times of cultural decline.

The individuals who are most qualified to discriminate between high and low can be expected to be the same as those who incline against categorical, unqualified statements about the specific ways in which goodness, truth, and beauty can be realized. Although a soundly traditional civilization manages to weed out many superficialities and perversities as clearly destructive of universal values and manages to define a general range wherein truly rewarding life may be sought, the ever-present danger of moral and cultural atrophy and routinization creates a permanent need for creativity and reinvigoration. A vital civilization always maintains continuity with the past, but it does so precisely to have the moral, intellectual, and aesthetic autonomy to seize emerging and perhaps unexpected opportunities. Disagreements about which specific actions, thoughts, and artistic creations best realize the good, the true, and the beautiful will of course always continue. Should a strong consensus among the most perceptive observers emerge in some particular case, it will not be because brilliant arguments are defeating deficient arguments in the abstract, but because superior experience is persuading by its own compelling example. Even the philosophical value of truth is a form of experience, experience conceptually articulated.

It should be acknowledged that intellectual effort forms an integral and indispensable part of the higher life of society. Pursuing truth is one of the imperatives of human existence. Goodness, truth, and beauty depend on one another for their respective development. Human action cannot proceed without reflection, without the person knowing in what kind of world he must act. But although reason contributes greatly to the enhancement of life, it is not ethically or aesthetically normative. Good philosophies of ethics and aesthetics are systematic conceptual accounts of how certain values are concretized in the practical and imaginative life, respectively. Logic, the study of thinking itself, describes the activity whereby philosophical truth is realized. It describes how man slowly works himself out of blindness and confusion and resists confining and distorting passion. The wisdom that philosophy may possess is made possible by thought that is kept open-minded by holding self-serving prejudice at bay. The likelihood of wise reflection improves the more the philosopher is able to do his work on the basis of a both broad and deep comprehension of life's higher possibilities, which assumes intimate familiarity with each of the aspects of life's higher potential. Single-minded preoccupation with either will, imagination, or reason to the serious detriment of the other two forms of our humanity warps the person's life and, thus, his thinking. Profound philosophy is such because it can observe human existence from the point of view of a well-rounded, many-sided appreciation of life's higher possibilities. It is in a position to reflect on the best of what humanity has wrought and thus to see all the rest in its proper perspective. The task of philosophy is to raise human experience into conceptual self-consciousness, which is to say that philosophy and the study of history ultimately coalesce.[3]

Objections by ahistorical rationalism to this view of philosophy are the protestations of a form of thinking that drains philosophy of our concrete, historical humanity. This kind of disembodied rationality has nothing to contribute to developing life's higher potentialities, except insofar as it violates its own epistemological premises and draws parasitically on the human experience that it disdains. Abstractionism creates more or less debilitating diversions from the possibilities that human existence actually offers. This happens not least when the "ideals" of rationalism become a basis for political activism. It is no coincidence that abstractionists typically satisfy a need for concreteness and warmth by means of utopian-idyllic imagination. That kind of imagination, too, avoids the world in which human beings must actually pursue their goals. It reinforces, indeed makes more enticing, the evasion of the terms and limits of man's historical existence—an attitude that is often linked with a strong will to power: The "ideal" mandates a remaking of society or the world, creating a sweeping justification for self-assertion.[4]

It is time to summarize these observations concerning history and universality. It has been argued that universality becomes known to

3. For an extensive exploration of the nature of philosophical rationality and the sense in which it is historical, see Ryn, *Will, Imagination and Reason*.

4. For a discussion of the connection between rationalism and dreamy imagination, see Ryn, "Imaginative Origins of Modernity"; and Irving Babbitt, *Literature and the American College* (New York: Houghton Mifflin, 1908; with an introduction by Russell Kirk, Washington, D.C.: National Humanities Institute, 1986), especially chs. 1 and 2.

man in concrete experience and that it has to be discovered by all individuals, generations, and societies for themselves. To the extent that universal values enter human life, they are their own reward and justification. The union of universality and particularity gives to experience a special magnetic quality. In the case of ethical responsibility the synthesis of the two fosters goodness and happiness; in the case of artistry, beauty; and in the case of reasoning, truth. Universality pulls humanity in its own direction by holding out the possibility of a more truly worthwhile existence. It challenges and tries to drive from the arena impulses that, while promising pleasure, are destructive of a more deeply satisfying quality of life. It is in this sense that experience can become normative—be its own standard. It should be evident from the above argument that this view hides no implication that human beings can arbitrarily decree what is to be good, true, or beautiful. The latter impose their own authority. Although the individual must creatively accommodate universal values in the context of a life that is particular and unique, these values can be realized only on their own terms. The special satisfaction that inheres in their realization cannot be forced or commanded, but once universality has come alive in experience, that experience is, by its very nature, normative.

For these reasons it is not the case that human experience could be evaluated as to its contribution to human fulfillment only with reference to a standard external to experience, such as principles of ahistorical reason. The latter can add nothing to the normative authority of universality as known in experience, only distort it or detract from it. Only experience itself can reveal whether particular principles reflect man's higher potential. *Experience that has ethical, intellectual, or aesthetic authority "passes judgment" on experience that is inherently less conducive to, or destructive of, the good, the true, and the beautiful.* Abstract principles can be more or less expressive of universality, but by themselves they are, precisely because of their lack of contact with the concrete, without normative authority. The rationality that creates them deliberately distances itself from the particulars of experience, hence also from the special quality of experience wherein universality is embodied.

Though this is not the place to go into the subject in depth, it should be stated that rationalists of various types are quite mistaken in assuming that abstract rationality is our only source of intellectual enlightenment. There exists a very different form of rationality, one that human beings use, more or less, all the time but of which the philosophers have been very slow to take full account. The rationality in question is more genuinely philosophical in that it is historical and therefore faithful to actual human experience. It does not involve forays into some postulated other world, unknown to human experience. It does not even consist of abstraction from the concrete—except in the special, limited sense that it gives *conceptual expression* to immediate human experience. This philosophical reason can speak with some familiarity of universality, for it seeks to encompass, penetrate, and articulate the full range of concrete life in which universality is manifested. This kind of rationality does not avoid the concrete and the particular in order to pursue some merely abstract coherence or certitude. It tries to be true to life by studying it from within. Philosophical reason is indistinguishable in the end from history—not the reifying, empiricist history of positivism or the nihilistic, incoherent "historicism" of postmodernism, but the lived history of humanity, which is simultaneous unity and diversity. This is the history that provides the material for genuinely philosophical reflection.

The effect of philosophical reasoning, therefore, is not to detach man from the world in which he must act or to dispose him to look for a perfection that bears no resemblance to the world of ordinary life. On the contrary, philosophy helps him see life as it is, in its higher potentiality as well as in its other aspects. It helps alert him to possibilities that are actually attainable. While abstract perfectionist moralism might lead to passing laws forbidding human foibles and idiosyncrasies, genuine philosophy, attuned as it is to the existing world, recognizes that in the attempt to address human problems it is necessary to have realistic expectations, make allowances for human weaknesses, and, most important, leave room for the higher life to find new forms. Abstract rationality sees no virtue in adapting to the historical world and consequently loses contact with the real needs and possibilities of human existence.

In a time of cultural dislocations and disruptions, when society is torn by competing preferences and traditions, ahistorical "idealistic" reasoning and imagination become particularly inadequate. Preferring to dwell beyond the concrete world, proponents of these approaches are incapable of acute perception of present circumstances and problems. Having failed to cultivate powers of historical observation and synthesis, they are not suited to the great tasks of reconstruction and reorientation. They are reduced to feebly echoing intellectual formulas, cleaving to utopian visions, or nobly decrying the times while being swept along in practice by the most powerful currents of the moment.

Social ferment and upheaval create a particularly strong need for historical perspective and discrimination and for creative reconstruction of the kind of continuities that connect man with the universal. The resources of the past must strengthen those who are acting, thinking, and imagining. They must be brought to bear on the problems and opportunities of the here and now, be taken up in new, perhaps radical-seeming initiatives. The task requires creative abilities out of the ordinary. The cheap and artificial universality of "idealistic" rationalism and imagination is more easily achieved and thus more popular among the intellectuals.

The fondness for a merely abstract universality is directly related to the tendency of specialization and fragmentation in the Western world. In science, the professions, business, education, the arts, and elsewhere, society is breaking into parts. A proliferation of different ways of thinking and acting that is not balanced by recognition and cultivation of a common human element is making it increasingly difficult for people to reach each other as fellow human beings. The fragmentation is due in large part to an inability to relate the particular to the universal. Instead of a dynamic and diversified whole we get, on the one hand, abstract, largely artificial and mechanical universality and, on the other hand, increasingly chaotic particularity. The relative orderliness or coherence of the particular specialty is no substitute for membership in the human race. Abstract universality is by its own definition incapable of synthesis with particularity. The merely external like-mindedness that it induces has no integral relationship with the parts that it is trying to order; it actually contributes to further specialization and fragmentation of life.

The philosophical reorientation that has here been called value-centered historicism is an attempt to overcome the artificial separation of universality and history. As should be clear by now, arguing for the possible synthesis of the two is not the same as denying or discounting the presence of evil, untruth, and ugliness in history. These are as real as their opposites. Indeed, their reality is more palpably obvious in concrete experience than in any abstractly stated propositions. Value-centered historicism calls for greater sensitivity to man's historical experience in the broadest sense and most especially to the immanent reality of goodness, truth, and beauty. The dualism of life that is expressed in such terms as eternal and transitory, infinite and finite, and universal and particular is a dialectical polarity and must not be understood as involving reified, separate, unrelated entities. The pairs exist in union as well as tension. The higher potentialities of life must be realized in tension with other potentialities. Ahistorical habits of thought and imagination are poorly attuned to this dynamic of actual human existence. If epistemology and the philosophy of universal values are to be reinvigorated, those habits must finally be broken.

CHAPTER TEN

The Unique Expression
of the Universal

As this study of unity and diversity moves to its conclusion it is appropriate to explore further the implications of the above philosophical argument for how we understand human creativity, the power which, other than forces beyond human control, ultimately shape the world. More should be said about what may be described as the medium of creativity: human personality. It is through their personalities that men apprehend and change the world. But no two persons are the same. Their histories are different, partly because of their own previous actions. Different individuals approach the world differently. Even in the life of a single individual no two moments or situations can be the same. What needs more attention is a question that has been addressed above in mostly rather general philosophical terms: How could individuals, in their uniqueness as human beings, give expression to something of universal significance? Must they not, in order to accomplish such a task, first go as far as they can in overcoming their individuality? In keeping with the dialectical nature of life, the answer is yes, and no—which will undoubtedly seem to both abstract universalists and postmodern multiculturalists a case of outrageous equivocation. But genuine philosophy does not approach life by imposing a rigid, ready-made intellectual scheme of explanation and by trying to explain away whatever does not fit. Philosophy tries to be guided by what life itself has to say.

The following argument about the subject of creativity and personality can be applied also to the lives of peoples and civilizations, and this book will end by indicating the implications of the reasoning for relations among them.

To define the issue of personality we may restate and extend previous arguments. Abstract universalism means, in practice, a lack of interest in and respect for individual human beings and groups in their distinctiveness and with their special needs and opportunities. It does not follow that postmodern "historicism" offers a humane alternative. True, we must recognize the inevitable historicity of human existence, its contextual and contingent character, but postmodernism turns even history into a meaningless notion by its frantic and therefore disingenuous denial of universality. Without some unity or "oneness" of human experience, no consciousness could exist. Without an element of continuity there could be no history, only disjointed, meaningless fragments. There could be no science, art, or philosophy—no civilization.

Postmodernists do at times at least approximate a sense of the uniqueness of persons. This groping awareness comes in part from their being strongly influenced, knowingly or unknowingly, by the romantic movement, which is still exercising great influence, though often in extreme and intellectually rather unproductive form. Romanticism was always prone to excess and extravagance, but in the Western world it did help sharpen an appreciation for the uniqueness of individuals. What debilitates postmodernism in its dominant strains is its compulsive insistence that life is individuality and nothing else. It contends that, because individual persons have different histories and can have only the perspectives that their backgrounds have made possible, they cannot share meaning but must always talk past each other. Fish and others are famously asserting that literary works are only "texts" understood differently by each reader.

When a movement denies something that actual human experience amply confirms, there is every reason to suspect dubious motives. In the case of postmodernism one recognizes an all too familiar wish, dating back at least as far as Rousseau, to be rid of every old prejudice of the human race, so that it becomes possible to indulge the desire of the moment without even having to have a bad conscience. Postmodernists are making illegitimate use of something that is quite true and that has long been known by serious students of historicist philosophy: that life is inescapably historical.[1] No two individuals can have identically the same perceptions and reactions. On the basis of this observation, which should be virtually self-evident to the philosophically educated person, postmodernists arbitrarily conclude that no genuine conversation, no sharing of experience is possible. We may grant, indeed, must grant, that each human being has a unique history and personality, but there is no reason, except bad theory, why this fact should preclude transpersonal meaning. If being shaped by particular historical circumstances ruled out understanding a person in a different situation, it would not be possible for a particular individual to understand himself from moment to moment, different as these are, to say nothing of understanding himself as he was long ago. But every person knows from experience that there is continuity of self and consciousness as well as discontinuity. A person is able, though sometimes with difficulty, to understand himself as he was at different stages of his life. This is the case also with members of the same family. Members of the same culture, too, often recognize themselves sufficiently in each other to be able to exchange meaning. The same is true, though perhaps to a lesser extent, even of people from different societies and cultures, provided they make the effort necessary really to acquaint themselves with another frame of reference.

Beyond the various and sometimes major obstacles to genuine communication, people intuit in themselves and each other a common humanity. Whatever the epistemological or aesthetic theories of philosophers and artists, in their actual work they assume themselves to be addressing human beings in general, not just themselves. This is an assumption without which philosophy and art would become pointless. Postmodernists deny transpersonal meaning but nevertheless write books, give lectures, and attend conferences. Their practice belies their theory. That they, too, engage in discourse and try to persuade others of the validity of their views is evidence that human consciousness has a universal dimension, both actual and potential, that cannot be plausibly denied.

---

1. Croce's *Story of Liberty* is uncompromising in its advocacy of historicism but also in its advocacy of universality.

In the field of morality, denials of universality have long been common in the Western world, but here, too, a more than subjective and transitory frame of reference is indicated by the implied importance of convincing others of the validity of those denials. The nihilist takes for granted that nihilism is not an idiosyncratic and arbitrary position but one on which reasonable people can agree after seriously considering the human moral predicament, which is thus assumed to be in some sense common to human beings. It is worth adding that the very intensity and fervor with which many nihilists deny moral universality suggests that to some extent they are trying to persuade themselves and are having difficulty freeing themselves of a sense that moral right is more than a subjective preference. Those who do struggle with conscience demonstrate that, whatever theory they embrace, they actually recognize the existence of a moral obligation that is both impersonal and pointedly and acutely personal. Though pangs of conscience are profoundly individual, a deep disturbance within the unique life's situation of a particular person, they would carry no weight, no authority, unless they were also felt to be somehow related to a concern for what is right for its own sake, that is, to a supraindividual imperative.

Before taking another step in explaining the sense in which uniqueness can become the bearer of the universals of goodness, beauty, or truth, it may be useful briefly to recapitulate earlier reasoning and adapt it to the present discussion. Advocates of both postmodernism and abstract universalism are trying to force upon us an artificial choice. If you want diversity and freedom, say the postmodernists, you must give up the notion of a common humanity and an ultimate standard of goodness, truth, or beauty. If you want unity and universal values, say the abstract universalists, you must disparage and try to overcome personal and cultural distinctiveness. Either/or! Left out because of philosophical deficiencies on both sides is the possibility of synthesis. Neither side will recognize that human moral, cultural, and intellectual life is a field of potentialities, affected by human choices, in which opposites struggle against each other but in which particularity and universality can also be in a relation of give and take that brings universality more fully to life. Indeed, the dialectic that articulates higher values is not between abstract entities but between the evolving uniqueness of particular persons and the goodness, truth, and beauty that they are able more or less successfully to bring to life in their very own circumstances. Real universality is the opposite of a procrustean bed whereby conformity is enforced; it is evolving potentiality that is to some extent wholly unpredictable. Neither are personal and other cultural identities like pebbles moving in the surf on a beach, distinct objects with a purely external and frictional relationship; they are the particulars of a living whole of inexhaustible richness. Universality and particularity are not terms for inanimate, separate phenomena. In their tension and union they are life itself, constituting the world of human beings.

Absorbing a great work of art may exemplify the union between the universal and the uniquely personal. To enter into the work is to explore potentialities of one's own self and of all humanity. The great artist makes us see aspects of our own existence that we could not see as clearly and deeply without him. No human being was ever engaged by a great poem, symphony, or painting without an intense feeling of personal involvement. This work deeply concerns *me*! Being addressed to no particular person, it nevertheless speaks directly to the individual. For this to happen the individual needs to be creative, capable, at least minimally, of recreating the work of the artist in his own circumstances. In the imagination, the person spontaneously adapts the work to his own life and general experience, letting it articulate and expand that personal sphere. Absorbing the work, the person makes it his own. His reactions, which are conditioned by *his* life, are those of nobody else.

Yet no one was ever drawn into a great work of art without assuming that it speaks not only to him but to any other person with the preparation to take it in. The reader of a superior novel does not feel alone but is, on the contrary, intuitively aware of other possible readers in the very moment of reading. They are, as it were, looking over the shoulder. This is no less the case if the book that the reader is holding in his hand is an old dusty volume that has not left the library for decades. He is in the reading of the novel representing humanity and sharing it with humanity. He senses humanity's excitement, its delight, its dread, or its chuckle along with his own. Though the rest of humanity is not crowding into his study, he feels its strong interest and its emotions along with his own. Without the presence of others the reader would find little meaning in the novel. He is anxious to bring his experience to the attention of other persons whom he expects to be receptive to and in need of the novel. Meaning is intensely personal, but it is meaningful precisely because it links unique individuality with universal humanity.

In a theater or concert hall, being part of an audience of whose reactions one is intensely aware together with one's own merely concretizes and strengthens the sense that absorbing a work of art is a communal experience as well as a very personal one. Being together with others in this manner is a decisive factor in making a people or a culture what it is. This communal dimension does not have to assume the form of a public gathering, but in the history of the human race it often has. The public performance or display of works of art has been essential in forming the sense of cohesion, belonging, distinctiveness, and pride of different peoples. One thinks, for example, of ancient Athenians gathered in an amphitheater for performances of Sophocles's three Theban plays, works already familiar to many in the audience but now taken in once more partly as a communal act of contrition and restored unity before the gods. The works of Homer had long shaped the Greek imagination. Does this mean that Athenians imagined, thought, and acted in unison? Obviously not. They and the Greeks were not as acutely conscious of the importance and the needs of human individuality as people would be in the Western world from the eighteenth and nineteenth century forward, but, then as now, particular persons reacted individually to a literary tradition.

The fine Canadian novelist Robertson Davies, who died in 1995, is also a notable commentator on literature and life. He writes perceptively on the role of "dreams" created by artists in both constituting and articulating the experience of a people or a culture, what an anthropologist might call the "tribe." The dream simultaneously gives the individual a sense of belonging and of personal enhancement. Commenting on the effects on himself of William Shakespeare's *A*

Midsummer Night's Dream, Davies writes that he recognizes himself in all the personages in the play:

> Because, you see, this is one of the very greatest dreams of the tribe, and whenever I see it I feel both immeasurably enriched in myself and also very much more a member of the tribe. Here, in the present, the past has spoken to me, as I know that it will speak to the future when I am no more.[2]

Great art, then, plays a multifaceted role in joining universality and particularity. Though this chapter is using art to illustrate the synthesis of the universal and the distinctive, the same dialectical relationship characterizes achievements of truth or goodness in the philosophical and moral life, respectively.

To continue using art as an illustration, an artistic experience is in a sense irreducibly personal and individual. Yet it may also, as we have seen, be a highly significant influence in the formation or expression of what may be called *a transindividual cultural consciousness.* This term does not refer to an apprehension of life unaffected by personal individuality; it signifies a special form of particularity, one that heightens the sense of belonging to a civilization, society, tribe, or family *at the very same time* that it heightens the sense of individual personal identity. Transindividual cultural consciousness is, like everything else in human life, a matter of more or less. It can be achieved only by effort and persistence. The higher the level on which it is realized, the more it joins immanence and transcendence. A great work of art can indeed be the special and indispensable treasure of a particular people, helping to form its unity and identity, but it can also become a treasure for all of mankind. In the very process of creating cultural distinctiveness and boundaries the great work does, in its humane significance, simultaneously break down those same boundaries among those who are capable of truly absorbing it, giving humanity a common frame of reference.

2. Robertson Davies, *One Half of Robertson Davies* (New York: Penguin Books, 1978), 147.

Some concrete literary examples will make the same point. Are modern Swedes and Scandinavians incapable of resonating to the tragedy of human blindness and arrogance in the play of *Oedipus* by an ancient Greek? Do the works of Shakespeare have nothing to say to a Frenchman? Is a German beyond grasping the world of Dostoyevsky? In short, is a European, Western literary culture impossible? To deny that possibility is to deny a historical fact, for such a culture, marked by diversity as well as unity, has indeed existed, and it shaped the imagination and conduct of many generations of Westerners. To some extent this culture still exists. Taking the same line of thinking further, are Chinese readers unable to identify with the romantic longings and anxieties of Emma Bovary? Are Americans unable to grasp the callousness and capriciousness of Hsi Men in *Chin P'ing Mei* (*Golden Lotus*)?

The experience of great art shows that the imagination permits people of very different backgrounds to share and be profoundly affected by particular visions. That an outstanding novel must be read differently by each person is evidence of the compatibility of unity and diversity. One of the effects of opening oneself up to the artistic treasures of the world is to become aware not only that life is perceived similarly by people of different times and places, but also that a sense of the universal and of the higher obligations of human beings is of the essence of the greatest artistic achievements. The latter bring a sense of elevation and consolation, capturing the grandeur as well as the suffering of humanity while giving it hope. For members of different cultures to cultivate their highest common ground is to heighten this awareness of the nature and purpose of human existence. As already indicated, the role of great art in synthesizing universality and particularity is analogous to that of great thought and great moral conduct.

Like individuals, peoples are deeply conditioned by their own past. They have distinctive outlooks because of it. But, like individuals, they are also carried beyond family, tribe, region, and nation by what is most deeply humane in their cultures. Indelibly imprinted with their own culture, they participate in the quest for the universal.

The dialectical and synthetical relationship between universality and particularity may be further explained in the most general terms. The good, the true, and the beautiful are in one sense only unfinished potentialities. They are qualities that an infinite number of not yet completed acts, thoughts, and works of art may have. But the good, the true, and the beautiful do at the same time already exist, as values that attract and spur human beings. These values have already been brought alive in countless acts, thoughts, and works of art—in loving, morally responsible behavior, wise books and lectures, outstanding poems and compositions. These creations are among the influences that, because they concretize the universal, inspire individuals to new creativity.

Do then universals exist, or do they not? Only in the splendid isolation of pure universality, shorn of all particularity, assert the antihistoricists; particulars have no value as such but merely reflect universality in a vague and distorted way. No, say historicists of the postmodern type, universals do not exist; all that exists are ultimately meaningless particulars that bring transitory idiosyncratic satisfaction to inescapably solitary individuals.

Both groups are mistaken. Consider the depth and aesthetical unity of a painting by Rembrandt. The universality of the work is inseparable from what is distinctive to Rembrandt, the person-painter. The same is true for a symphony by Beethoven. Without the unique marks of his particular genius, the symphony would not be what it is. But surely, says the proponent of abstract universalism, what is truly great about a work of art stems from the artist's having emptied himself of his own personality and having thereby become the conduit for universality. The postmodernist, for his part, protests that art can express only the sensibilities of historically bound personalities and that universality has nothing to do with the work. The answer to both is that, in great works of art—as in great works of morality and thought—universality and particularity cannot be themselves without each other.

In creating the mentioned works the artists were truly themselves, more so perhaps than at any other time. Nothing could divert them from their vision-in-the-making. Letting themselves be diverted would have been a betrayal of their innermost selves. Rembrandt and Beethoven painted and composed as only they could, yet they were more than just themselves. Within their essential personalities was a self that demanded their very best. They could not arbitrarily decide when to call their works finished. Something deep within them, something that they still could not control but only serve, demanded satisfaction. A transindividual, universal imperative was concretized in intensely personal demands on self. Until the completion of the works, the anxiety and pain of creation had to continue. In the finished works, personality and universality came together, not as separate elements mixed like oil and water, but as forces in great need of each other, implicated in each other from beginning to end.

Just as the personality of the artist and the aesthetical imperative come together in works of art, so are particularity and universality joined in the motif or subject of what is artistically expressed. This may be most easily seen in the portrayal of human beings. Compare a portrait by Rembrandt to the drawing of a face in a cartoon or advertisement. The former sees so much more deeply into the human condition, has so much more universality, precisely because it captures human individuality with great penetration. The cartoon or illustration are incapable of rendering intense individuality, can offer only simplistic generality; the portrait by Rembrandt shows unique personality and through it the universal.

That something individual might deepen our sense of the universal seems unintelligible only if one insists on thinking of particularity and universality as if they were separate phenomena and not mutually implicated in each other. Here, as in other places, the "blockhead" must yield to the philosophical mind. To the latter there is nothing contradictory in what was just said about a portrait by Rembrandt, because— and this should be carefully noted—only in personal uniqueness does universal humanity come alive.

Perhaps it should be said explicitly that art which leaves a lasting and major mark and lifts human existence for large numbers of people is not common. Though all art above a certain level answers in some way, however limited, to the description previously given, most artists never create works of indubitable general interest. Some follow transitory fashion or occupy themselves with trivia. Some who do have substantial creative gifts use them to express perverse, degrading visions without redeeming value. Yet others put their artistic ability in the service of nonaesthetic, practical desires, such as the pursuit of fame or money, sell themselves to the highest bidder or pander to the current arbiters of what is art. Especially in times of cultural debility and confusion works of full-bodied, penetrating, proportionate, and centered vision, the kind that enriches the life of all humanity, may be recognized for what they are only by a few.

We have come to the very center of universality: the individual person. Individuality is needed for universality to be embodied. The creativity of the person, whether moral, aesthetical, or intellectual, holds the key to elevating human existence. There is no substitute for individuals straining to make the best of their own lives. The gist of what has been argued here about personhood is that, for a human being to give the best he can, he must cultivate his own personality— not those potentialities that rebel against the good, the true, and the beautiful but those that can help give fresh expression to them. By trying to be truly himself the person makes the contribution that only he can make and that the world most needs from him; he enriches it with the distinctiveness of his own personality, ennobled by service to the universal. Paradoxical though it sounds, it is in the *intensification* of personal uniqueness of that kind that the universal is realized.

The intensification of personhood is not an obstacle to community. On the contrary, it is this special form of individualism that most fundamentally binds human beings together. Members of soundly formed and inspired groups appreciate other members not because they are essentially the same as the other members but because their diverse personalities enrich and strengthen the group. Individuals are liked for who they are in their distinct humanity. They help satisfy varied needs. What has been said about single individuals developing their own identity applies equally to associations, societies, and cultures. Subdivisions of mankind made up of individuals who strive to cultivate their own higher humanity pose no threat to other groups that aspire to the same goal. Members of the one group recognize that society can only benefit from a proliferation of groups devoted each in its own way to the higher purposes of human life.

It goes without saying that no association or society conforms fully to this account of group-life at its best. Because of the flaws of human nature, the social cohesion just described is always a matter of more or less. The ethos of some groups is very different: stale, provincial, oppressive, and positively destructive of the higher individuality. Some are held together by rigid authority, other external pressure, or calculating egotism. In such a group or in a society dominated by a similar ethos the person who is trying properly to be himself has no choice but to rebel for the sake of the higher life.

For the cultivation of the spirit of universality to be possible in varied historical circumstances subdivisions of mankind must be able to pursue their distinctiveness and protect it against wanton subversion or external threat. A respect for local, national, or cultural identity that springs from a concern for life's higher values benefits humanity as well as the particular society. The proper cultivation of what is distinctive to the subdivision enriches mankind locally, nationally, and globally; it helps *harmonize* diversity. The appreciation for diversity as a potential expression of universality is an important component of what has here been called cosmopolitan humanism. It is inherently a force for peace.

The proper and necessary cultivation of uniqueness, then, must not be confused with a romantic or more frankly egotistical pursuit of an indiscriminate, undisciplined, anarchic uniqueness, for example, of the postmodernist variety. The self-realization that has been advocated here is the medium for the realization of goodness, truth, and beauty, which means that this kind of cultivation of self is indistinguishable from a strong sense of direction. This is the case even though the values governing the quest are forever in need of clarification and rearticulation and protection from attack.

A society built on this kind of understanding of universality will want to grant the greatest possible leeway for individuals and groups to find their own way in order to ensure that new, perhaps wholly unexpected ways of expressing the universal will not be stifled. Because people of less worthy motives will take advantage of available liberties, the amount of freedom that a society can allow its members will depend upon the extent to which freedom is responsibly exercised.

The argument of this book does not assume that some particular configuration of cultural identities is the only "natural" one and must be maintained forever, so that, for example, the survival of certain nations is always ensured. No identities can be perpetuated that do not from within themselves generate a capacity for continuity and reinvigoration. Some national or international cultures will peter out—for lack of interest, as it were. Once vigorous and influential, they will be forgotten or absorbed into other cultures. Some societies will succumb to more aggressive and powerful societies.

Even among those societies that are full of creativity and verve there is some interpenetration, which means that no particular cultural identity is like a watertight compartment. Again, cosmopolitan humanism forms part of any civilized society. No societies or persons are just themselves. This is chiefly because of their history. A Swede is a Swede, but also, specifying some of his national traits and origins, a Scandinavian, a German, an Englishman, a Protestant, a Roman Catholic, an ancient Roman, an ancient Greek, and an ancient Hebrew. He is a representative of Western civilization. Nevertheless, a great variety of related strands of history together with a genetic biological heritage have congealed into a distinctive Swedish nationality that has endured over the generations.

Only in the intensification of what is distinctive does the latter show its vitality and value. The loss of such concentration and the spread of a diffuse, vapid multiplicity of influences signifies the dissipation of culture.

History is replete with peoples who out of their own past have created a nationality or larger cultural identity of unusual creativity and staying power. They make an enduring mark, become a model and inspiration for others. Their members find satisfaction and pride in being who they are. They celebrate their own distinctiveness and strengths. They want to transmit their identity to their posterity. A cultural entity of this kind may still begin to lose its vitality, not because its resources are spent, but because, for whatever reason, its elites neglect their traditions and the task of transmitting their heritage through continuous rearticulation and development. When this entity devolves into decadence all of mankind loses. The flabbiness and disorientation of a deteriorating culture is no asset to anybody, in fact, may do great damage to other societies before the culture finally dissolves.

When some societies lose their traditional identity and fade away the loss to the people most immediately affected and to mankind as a whole is profound. The deleterious repercussions are far-reaching. Important achievements that might have benefited many people are lost and can be recovered only in some new form, if at all, and only by great and protracted effort and after much needless deprivation and suffering.

It hardly needs saying that all traditional societies have notable weaknesses and that some are much less admirable or humane than others. Much time has already been spent in this book explaining that a properly traditional society is always trying to select and extend the best in its own traditions and to discard whatever blocks the development of its higher potentialities. This is the same effort that pulls different societies and cultures toward a common center.

As we have seen, today many want to replace the diversity of historically evolved peoples and civilizations with a "universal" global culture. They do not grieve any lost historical opportunities of the kind just mentioned, for their view of humanity is flat and prosaic. To these globalists, a good society or world is one in which all live in the same way, the way that the globalists themselves deem to be superior. They do not recognize the conceit of the presumption that the world should be transformed according to their own ideas, for they have little awareness of the depth, complexity, and richness of humanity, formed as it is by histories extending in complex ways back to the beginning of time. These globalists cannot see any need for human beings to cultivate their distinctive origins. After all, the model of society that they advocate is recognized by all enlightened persons as the one for which mankind has always been seeking. What is cultural distinctiveness but an obstacle to achieving the desirable social arrangements and ideological homogeneity? The efforts of the globalists to substitute a new world order of their own for historically rooted societies will efface not only what they may think of as the quaint and superficial "charm" of various traditions, but will gut mankind's deeper, shared, though highly diverse, humanity. These efforts will rob mankind of a rich source of value and self-understanding. They could benefit only people who have something to gain from others losing their creativity, strength, and self-confidence.

The notion of synthesis of universality and particularity that has been advanced in this book will be hard to comprehend only to the extent that artificial, abstract intellectual constructs are allowed to take the place of the living reality of human life. If actual human experience is taken seriously as evidence, nothing could be more plausible, more real, than that the universal and the particular, the impersonal and the personal can become one and indistinguishable.

Though the examples and illustrations in this concluding chapter have been taken disproportionately from art and individual creativity, the general philosophical thesis regarding universality and particularity has the widest possible scope and import. The conclusions reached are directly relevant to the question raised at the very beginning of the book: whether it might be possible for societies and cultures in the twenty-first century to avoid conflict and achieve some mutual understanding and respect. The answer is that movement toward a more than perfunctory and short-lived unity in diversity is indeed possible and that working toward this goal is fully compatible with cultures, societies, and individuals retaining their selfhood and developing their own distinctiveness. Unity can be achieved *through* diversity.

That a different kind of pursuit of the personal and the particular is wholly inimical to this goal has already been made clear. The danger is obvious from the power of man's lower inclinations to undermine what holds human existence together and makes it worth having. As divorced from a concern about the universal, a pursuit of personal or national distinctiveness can produce self-aggrandizement and ruthlessness and throw societies into domestic or international conflict. The chronic human weaknesses and foibles that break life apart and aggravate tensions are too familiar to need listing. At their worst, the personal and the particular can not only destroy relations among human beings but dissolve individual personality itself. Madness is sometimes self-inflicted. In some of its forms, postmodernism can be seen as conducive to an obliteration of individual identity—a prescription for madness. A flat denial of universality is a recipe for personal, national, and international disintegration, chaos, and conflict. Abstract universalism, for its part, not least the type advocated by the new Jacobinism, can be as destructive of civilized order and contribute as much to conflict, because it cares much less about self-discovery and self-direction than it does about imposing its allegedly universal principles on others.

The philosophy that has been offered here in the place of these dangerous alternatives is value-centered historicism, of which cosmopolitan humanism and a special type of multiculturalism are integral parts. Most generally, this philosophy proposes a way of thinking about universality and particularity, and in so doing it advances a view of our higher humanity. More specifically, it offers an understanding of the preconditions for peace and respect among individuals and peoples. In view of the globalization that can be expected to continue in the twenty-first century, this book has been an attempt to demonstrate the urgency and necessity of cultivating the highest common human ground, which is the same as cultivating individual distinctiveness at the highest level.

Peace will not emerge spontaneously. The argument here has run in precisely the opposite direction. There are no shortcuts, such as narrowly political or economic measures, to creating genuine respect and friendliness among peoples. There is no substitute for different individuals, societies, and cultures undertaking the protracted and difficult moral, cultural, and intellectual efforts that will moderate their own self-indulgence, strengthen their nobler aspirations, and let them glimpse the higher life that belongs to all humanity.

Appendix

The following is a translation from Chinese by Nong Cheng of Yue Daiyun's foreword to Claes Ryn's Unity through Diversity, *published by Beijing University Press in 2001 and based on the lecture series originally delivered at Beijing University.*

Yue Daiyun is one of China's best-known intellectuals. Professor of Chinese and comparative literature at Beijing University, she is also president of the Chinese Comparative Literature Association and editor in chief of Cross-cultural Dialogues. *She was director of the Institute for Chinese and Comparative Culture at Beijing University. She is known for her strong interest in Chinese culture in relation to questions of globalization.*

Faced with the unavoidable tide of globalization, can the cultural diversity of thousands of years of human history be preserved? How can it endure and develop? Some people hold that the liberal democracy constructed in the West is a universal value and that its universality and superiority are sufficient to qualify it as the model for all cultures across the world. But this position raises doubts in the minds of others: What about our own culture? Should it be merged into the common model and gradually dwindle until it disappears and survives only in tourist commercials? Will emphasis on universality cause cultural hegemony for a certain culture? Will emphasis on particularity block people from communicating with one another and cause disintegration? In recent years I have been looking for answers to these questions. I found that a historian in early ancient China suggested, "Harmony among different elements is productive, while homogeneity is not." Confucius said, "The Gentleman aims at harmony among heterogeneous factors rather than total agreement; the mean person does the opposite." For this reason, it is always a goal in Chinese culture to emphasize differences and strive for their harmonious coexistence. But how this ideal can be connected with our own present reality and assist in dealing with our troubles remains for me a problem.

In this state of confusion I fortunately encountered the Swedish scholar Claes Ryn. That I encountered him was no accident. Doing research on the intellectual controversies caused by the introduction into China of a variety of Western ideas during the May Fourth period, I felt deeply that the Xucheng [*Critical Review*] school centered around the journal by that name, which wanted to "develop the Chinese national essence and integrate Western thought into it," was indeed original with regard to the relationship between Chinese culture and Western culture. It exerted an indelible influence at that time. I discovered that this school was greatly influenced by Professor Irving Babbitt at Harvard, who advocated the New Humanism and was also an admirer of Confucianism and Buddhism. Further investigation revealed that there is a research institute [the National Humanities Institute] that promotes Babbitt's cultural legacy in contemporary America. The institute publishes an academic journal called *Humanitas,* and its editor is Claes Ryn, a professor at the Catholic University of America.

I could not wait to meet him. I invited him to the sixth meeting of the Chinese Comparative Literature Association and International Academic Symposium that was held in Chengdu. Ryn presented an excellent paper titled "Unity in Diversity: On Cultivating the Common Ground," which provoked much lively discussion at the conference and beyond. In spite of a number of conversations with him, I felt there was much left to discuss. That is why I was very pleased to be able to invite Professor Ryn to give a lecture series at Beijing University. This book is based on those lectures.

In his lectures Ryn criticizes the desire to make the whole world over according to a single model. He refers to such neoconservatives in the United States as Allan Bloom as new Jacobins, arguing that they, like the Jacobins of the French Revolution, "want to mobilize politically and even militarily in behalf of what they deem good for the peoples of the world." He points to their "lack of interest in or resentment of historically formed cultural particularity and their belief that a certain political doctrine is entitled to hegemony, nay, monopoly."

What the new Jacobins actually want to do is impose their own subjective preferences on others and subjugate other nations. Also, Ryn stresses that "variety that is not humanized by concern for the higher life but that expresses mere arbitrary willfulness or eccentricity can give rise to great volatility and worse." As Edmund Burke says, "Men of intemperate minds cannot be free. Their passions forge their fetters." If human beings do not feel that life has any deeper meaning, they will increasingly look for instant gratification, following the strongest impulse and indulging the pleasure of the moment without regard to anything else.

Professor Ryn argues that we should strive for the higher life and the fulfillment of our humanity and improve our existence as much as possible. In so doing we should impose powerful constraints on our selfishness and pride. Besides needing humility, self-restraint, and sincere mutual respect, human beings should be aware that they share a higher humanity that appears in different forms. Our humanity is rooted in different cultural soils and is nourished by the best nutrients of those cultures. A culture that is really strong is not stagnant and does not ossify into certain rigid patterns. Rather, it must continually develop to meet the needs of different times and places and become a dynamic power of universal life. This belief coincides with the basic views of the New Humanism advocated by Babbitt, which has been inherited and developed by Ryn. The problem of the relationship between the universal and the particular, which has been discussed since Plato and Aristotle, here receives further illumination. Ryn's lectures reminded me from time to time of the tradition of "harmony among different elements" in Chinese culture, and he gave me a new understanding of the problem.

Ryn's lectures are very rich, far more so than I have been able to indicate here. It must be noted that his lectures aroused extensive and penetrating discussion among the students. The lectures will surely leave a deep imprint upon the scholarly careers of many of them. Regrettably, it is not possible in this space fully to record the intellectual excitement and enthusiasm of the discussion and questioning. It is a great pity that such an account cannot be included here, and I am afraid that this omission is not easily remedied.

Index

Abstractionism, 75, 111, 113
  and Aristotle, 64, 65
  modern, 75
Aristotle, 13, 14, 22, 68, 70, 72, 137
  and abstractionism, 64, 65
  attention to the concrete in philoso-
    phy of, 74
  Nicomachean Ethics, 74, 104
  and normative primacy of concrete
    experience, 104
  and particularity as a guide to the
    universal, 75
  perceived similarity with John Locke,
    75
  rationality of incorrectly perceived as
    ahistorical, 75
  and rejection of philosophical
    modernity, 70
  and suitability of different forms of
    rule, 49, 50
Art
  as union of the universal and the
    personal, 122–27
Augustine, Saint, 72

Babbitt, Irving, 15n, 27n1, 77n
  and Buddhism, 41
  on Burke and the past as a force upon
    the present, 28
  and Burke's "moral imagination," 44,
    80
  and Confucianism, 41
  on humanitarian schemes and "will
    to power," 52n6
  on the "inner check," 40, 41
  and metaphysics of the One and the
    Many, 8

  and "more complete positivism," 43
  and "New Humanism," 8n, 136, 137
  notion of the universal, 80
  opposition to abstractionism, 82
  on rationalism and the imagination,
    113n4
  and role of philosophy in morality,
    41
  and significance of art in understand-
    ing human condition, 44
Bach, J. S., 106
Bacon, Francis, 77
Baker, James
  on universal applicability of enlight-
    enment ideals, 51, 52n6
Baldacchino, Joseph,
  on value-centered historicism of
    Edmund Burke, 59n
Barth, Karl
  and "otherness of God," 9, 62
Beethoven, Ludwig von, 106, 126
Bell, Daniel
  on the "end of history," 50n
Bennett, William, 48
Bergson, Henri, 94–95
Blockheadedness, 65
  defined, 64
Bloom, Allan,
  critical of historicism, 58, 136
  as disciple of Strauss, 51
  and Jacobin notion of universality, 54
  as neoconservative, 48
  and perceived democracy of Plato, 70
  on superiority of democracy, 51
  and universal applicability of Ameri-
    can principles, 50, 51
Brooks, David, 52n5

on purpose of historical science and
culture, 27
on relationship between "the
economical" and the ethical, 87n
on societal consciousness of the past,
26
Cropsey, Joseph, 73n
Culture
cultural interaction as basis for peace,
12
deterioration of, 130, 131

Dante Alighieri, 106
Davies, Robertson
on dreams, 123, 124
Democracy, 5
alleged appropriateness for all
societies, 48
difference between constitutional and
plebiscitarian forms, 53, 54
Framers' suspicion of, 53
neo-Jacobin advocacy of, 49
Dewey, John
importance of historical continuity in
works of, 94–96
perceived critique of postmodernism,
95
pragmatism of, 94, 95n8
Rousseauistic notion of togetherness
in thought of, 97
sentimental humanitarianism of, 96
and value-centered historicism, 95
Dhammapada, 15, 41n3
Diversity
appreciation for as a force for peace,
129
guided by universal human element,
44
mutual requirement of unity and, 29
not obliterated by philosophy of e
pluribus unum, 55
not a threat to unity, 10
possibility of unity in, 18
value of, 1
Dostoyevsky, Fyodor, 125
Dryzek, John, 97

Ecumenism, 38
Education
analogy with moral/intellectual
maturing of society, 100–103
classical/Greek notion of (schole), 32
modern reluctance to include moral
self-discipline in, 32, 33
purpose of, 105
Elites
deterioration of culture due to failure
to transmit heritage, 130, 131
leadership role of, 36
need to live up to standards of
cosmopolitan humanism, 37
need to set examples for own society,
39
power of increased by egalitarianism,
37
respect for other cultures, 38
Enlightenment
French, 75
need to revise thinking of, 35
refusal to accept traditional view of
human nature, 31
unsatisfactory understanding of social
international order, 31
Equality
as preeminent Western value of
twentieth century, 36
Eudaimonia, 13, 101
Experience, 85, 86
can become normative, 114
good, true, beautiful discerned in, 89
impossible to evaluate from external
principles, 114
narrow empiricist concept of, 85
"passes judgment" on less perfect
form of experience, 114
as primary normative authority, 104
understood only in light of universality, 86

Federalist, The
on the purpose of government
institutions, 53
First World War, 25
Fish, Stanley, 3, 119

Humility
  different from pursuit of mediocrity,
    39
Huntington, Samuel
  on commonality between civiliza-
    tions, 46
  rejects "universalist" moral claims,
    47, 48

Ideals
  dangers of abstract ideals forming
    basis of political activism, 113
  dangers of disconnection from
    historical experience, 107
Idiosyncratic society, 3
  described, 106, 109
Imagination
  ahistorical character of, 77
  connection with rationalism, 113n4
  and escape from reality, 76–78
  essential role of in integrating history
    with personal experience, 28
  interaction with the intellect, 76–
    78
  mentioned, 5
  and moral evaluation of human
    experience, 108
  related to avoidance of historicity of
    human existence, 76
Individualism
  not an obstacle to community, 128
  and Romanticism, 119
  and universality, 118, 128
Intuition, 24n
  relation of philosophical rationality
    to, 63n
Islam, 13

Jacobinism
  and rights of man, 9
  and universalism, 49, 52, 54
  French Jacobins, 49, 61
  See also Neo-Jacobins
James, William, 41n3
Jay, John, 53n7
Jesus of Nazareth, 14, 22, 38

Kirk, Russell, 113n4
Krauthammer, Charles, 48
Kristol, William, 48
  on what ails conservatism, 52n5

Leander, Folke, 27n1
Liberalism, 67, 68
Lindbom, Tage, 3, 90
Locke, John
  comparison with Aristotle, 75
  imaginative thinking of, 77
  Second Treatise, 78

Machiavelli, Niccolò
  criticism of the ideal as guide to
    political morality, 82, 83
MacIntyre, Alasdair, 70
Madame Bovary
  Emma Bovary in, 125
Madison, James, 53n
Marx, Karl, 77
  Das Kapital, 78
Mill, John Stuart, 77
Modernity
  false choice between modernity and
    premodernity, 80, 81
Moralism
  antihistoricist tendency to detach
    from political life, 82
  and evasion of concrete moral
    obligations, 83, 84
Morality
  and "enlightened" self-interest, 57
  experiential content of in different
    societies, 39
  moral reality as preconceptual, 110n
  relegated to private sphere in modern
    Western society, 33
  universal values apprehended in
    specific moral actions, 90
Mozart, Wolfgang Amadeus, 106
Multiculturalism, 6
  postmodern refusal to recognize
    universality, 9
  postmodern multiculturalism and
    neo-Jacobinism, 56–58

Neo-Jacobins
  advocacy of universality, 60, 61
  analysis of, 54n9
  belief in "abstract universalism" of
    United States, 55
  claim reason as basis of universalism,
    52
  differences with Framers, 50, 55
  disregard for historical particularity,
    51, 55
  inspired by Straussian antihistoricism,
    59
  and Platonic view of universality, 55
  as reaction to postmodernism, 60
  self-identification with Plato consid-
    ered, 52
  and will to power, 52, 57
Nasr, S. H., 3, 90
Natural law
  and use in understanding universality,
    110
Neoconservatives
  ahistorical notion of universality, 49
  distinguished from traditional
    American or European forms, 49
  influenced by Strauss, 48
  similarities with French Jacobins, 49
  and universal principles, 49
  and virtue, 49
Neo-Thomism, 9
Nietzsche, Friedrich Wilhelm
  "slave morality" condemned by, 39
Nihilism
  denial of moral universality, 121
  and postmodernism, 2
Nirvana, 15, 42
Novak, Michael, 48
  and divine sanction of democracy,
    49

Particularism
  "historicist," 9
Particularity,
  historical, 7, 84
  as manifestation of universality, 1
  relationship with universality. See
    Universality

as vehicle for goodness, truth, beauty,
  27
Peace
  cultural interaction as basis for, 12
  moral and cultural preconditions of,
    2, 5, 11, 20, 21, 37, 133
  not advanced by superficial reporting
    in media, 46, 47
  prospects for related to reemergence
    of Western view of human nature,
    17, 18
  served by cosmopolitanism, 26, 36
  as union of universality and particu-
    larity, 5
  Western prescriptions for, 12
Philosophy
  coalesces with study of history, 113
  Greek and Roman, 13, 14
Plato, 3, 72, 137
  adapted by neo-Jacobins, 56
  and ahistorical nature of the good, 68
  alleged ahistorical rationality of, 75
  attention to the concrete in philoso-
    phy of, 74
  aversion to political participation, 82
  claimed by neoconservatives as an
    authority, 49, 52
  and democracy, 56
  and "democratic man" (The Republic),
    33, 34
  notion of political virtue of, 83n3
  perceived similarity with Rousseau,
    75
  perception of as democrat in disguise
    (Bloom), 70
  Seventh Letter, 82
  understanding of the "One" and the
    "Many," 7, 68
  universalism of, 52, 56, 70
Pluralism, 67
Podhoretz, Norman, 48
Positivism
  inadequate for study of morality, 43
  need to replace with philosophy
    respectful of man's inner life, 43
Postmodernism
  critique of rationalism, positivism, 18

About the Author

CLAES G. RYN is Professor of Politics and Founding Director of the Center for the Study of Statesmanship at the Catholic University of America. He also has taught at the University of Virginia and Georgetown University. He gave the Distinguished Foreign Scholar Lectures at Beijing University in 2000 and has visited China many times at the invitation of leading academic institutions, including the Chinese Academy of Social Sciences. He was named Honorary Professor at Beijing Normal University. His many books include *Democracy and the Ethical Life*, *America the Virtuous*, and *Will, Imagination, and Reason*.